/* **TRANSFORM** YOUR TECHNICAL
KNOWLEDGE INTO **POWERFUL MESSAGES** */

BE A
NERD
THAT
TALKS
GOOD

A MESSAGESPECS BOOK BY

JOEL BENGE

www.messagespecs.com

MessageSpecs and the spectacles logo are registered trademarks of MessageSpecs LLC

ISBN: 979-8-9912278-0-3 (paperback)
ISBN: 979-8-9912278-1-0 (ebook)
ISBN: 979-8-9912278-2-7 (hardcover)
ISBN: 979-8-9912278-3-4 (audiobook)

Printed in Columbia, MD

Library of Congress Control Number: 2025906631

Ordering Information:
Special discounts are available on quantity purchases by corporations, associations, and others. For details, contact publisher@messagespecs.com

Publisher's Cataloging-in-Publication Data:
Names: Benge, Joel, 1976- .
Title: Be a nerd that talks good : transform your technical knowledge into powerful messages / Joel Benge.
Description: Columbia, MD : MessageSpecs, 2025. | Series: MessageSpecs books ; 1. | Includes bibliographic references. | Includes 92 color illustrations, diagrams, and photos. | Summary: A practical guide to improving technical communication, this book introduces messaging frameworks based on classical rhetoric, modern psychology, and communication theory. Aimed at technical professionals, it offers tools to clarify and align messaging for marketing, branding, and team collaboration across technology-driven organizations.
Identifiers: LCCN 2025906631 | ISBN 9798991227827 (hardcover) | ISBN 9798991227803 (pbk.) | ISBN 9798991227810 (ebook) | ISBN 9798991227834 (audiobook)
Subjects: LCSH: Communication of technical information. | Business communication. | Communication in organizations. | Communication in marketing. | BISAC: BUSINESS & ECONOMICS / Business Communication / General. | BUSINESS & ECONOMICS / Marketing / General. | TECHNOLOGY & ENGINEERING / Technical Writing.
Classification: LCC T10.5 B46 2025 | DDC 302.2--dc23
LC record available at https://lccn.loc.gov/2025906631

Table of Contents

For my physician father and artist mother.

For my wife, who always has my back (sometimes shaking her head in disbelief).

For my son, who helped me create my first card game when he was only eight years old.

And, of course, for the developers, technical founders, product marketers, and other nerds!

Introduction(s)

The "Blank Stare" Moment

I think every technical founder, practitioner—even every tech marketer—has experienced it. You're giving a demo or talking about your tech—and you see the audience's attention drain away. Or you've stood up a new marketing asset—and gotten no traffic at all.

You did everything right—included all the talking points and background information, opened with the business case, and used "just the right amount" of graphics. Still, no one is picking up what you're putting down.

You may be telling yourself, "Some people are just born communicators and I'm not," or "It's not me—it's them," or "If I just dumb things down just a little...." Don't listen to those voices.

Every technical communicator has experienced this at some point. It's not your audience's fault—and it's not yours.

Why do the blank stares happen? What to do about them? And how do nerds like us overcome our tendency to either overwhelm our audience with detail or dumb things down?

That's what we're going to tackle together in this book.

This Isn't a "Marketing Book"

You won't find the answers to mapping the customer journey, identifying the ideal customer profile (ICP), or setting up an ABM/GTM/PLG/BLAH[1] strategy. (Though I will say that efforts in such areas will be greatly improved if you do read and follow the advice in this book.)

But maybe you're thinking, "Joel, this book is literally listed in the marketing book category. WTF?"

Yeah, about that. I didn't write this book to turn you into a marketer. What I'm about to share are the thought processes and models I've used—influenced by my technical background—in *my* marketing career. My goal is to help you uncover deeper truths about why, as a technical communicator, you are doing what you do and why others should listen to you.

In the end, I hope to help you create a foundation for technical communications (even marketing) that goes beyond mere tactics and playbooks—from one nerd to another.

I'll be borrowing from some of the greatest minds in classical philosophy and psychology—along with modern neuroscience and the entertainment industry—to rock your technical messaging world. Stuff like:

- Tapping into ancient philosophy to find a balance between the discrete persuasion modes of emotion, logic, and credibility.

- Using the neuropsychology of an audience to give them exactly the words they need at the right time.

- Playing a few hands of cards (with the deck stacked in your favor).

Along the way, we'll explore practical (and fun) ways of engaging with both technical and creative teams to create messaging that sticks and scales.

So, come along, nerds, tech wizards, and even you marketing

---

[1] Account-based marketing, go-to-market, product-led growth, and boring-long-as-heck strategies, respectively.

gurus—it's time to give your messaging a major upgrade and transform the way you talk tech.

But First, a Story

Before I help you tell yours, I'd like to tell you my story. Like any epic transformation tale (*Star Wars*, *Back to the Future*, Nickelodeon's *Rugrats*, etc.), it has three discrete parts.[2] Buckle up.

From Slime to Security

I've always considered myself a bit of a performer. My first job in high school was wearing a six-foot rat costume at a national entertainment chain restaurant where a kid could be a kid.[3] My final summer job was at a regional theme park, working with producers from Florida to create a stage mashup of the Nickelodeon network's greatest hits—physical challenges, pie fights, and green slime (of course). I entered college with a theater scholarship and visions of Oscars and Tonys dancing in my head.

Somewhere in the middle of my sophomore year in college, I figured it was time to get an actual job and make some actual money. This was before the dot-com bubble deflation of the late 1990s. I found myself working in technical support at a video game company. Believe me, you haven't lived until you've worked customer service on Christmas morning. ("Your game RUINED Christmas!")

But, through that job, I learned how to listen to customers and quickly diagnose their challenges—crafting a technical explanation at the level that matched their aptitude and solved their problems, set their holidays right, and got them the hell off the phone so I could go back to playing *Doom*.

---

2   For an interesting look at "The Rule of Three," check out chapter 4.

3   BEST ... JOB ... EVER! Nothing says "children's entertainment" better than a high schooler in a fur suit, pantomiming a happy birthday dance, while you and your friends stuff your faces with pizza and plunk coins into video game machines.

Fast forward through the help desk, system admin, network operations, Security Operations Center (SOC), and IT compliance roles, and I found myself squarely in my thirties wondering where all the pizza, cake, and games had gone.

Uncle Sam Comes Knocking

A chance lunch with a family friend pointed me toward an open position in the U.S. government. I applied for a security and compliance analyst position with the newly formed Department of Homeland Security (DHS). They took one look at my résumé and the hiring manager asked whether I was interested in a different position—communications manager.

"What's the difference," I asked, "between compliance and communications?"

"One lives in Microsoft Excel and the other in Word," was the reply. I figured my partial liberal arts background could serve me well there.

So, I found myself working for the chief information security officer at DHS as the principal cybersecurity communications manager. I spent my days coordinating cyber policy and strategy communications across the various departments, managing data calls for the executive secretariat's office, and writing the annual "change your password as frequently as you change your underwear" cybersecurity awareness messages.

That role laid the foundation for skipping the technical nonsense and getting to the point, when it came to presenting technical information.

Tech Startups and Tabletop Games

Fast forward nearly seven years. I was at another chance lunch meeting with the same manager who had hired me at DHS. He had recently left his White House position as a national security advisor on cybersecurity, completed his PhD, and launched a startup. But he found it challenging to quickly explain how his product worked and how it fit into customers' lives.

I asked him for his pitch. The tech was cool, but the story left something to be desired.

He invited me to join the founding team as product-evangelist-cum-marketing-director. "I don't know anyone who can tell a technical story like you can, Joel," he told me. I wasn't sure I believed him, but the pace of government work was wearing thin and I accepted.

Together, we redefined the product and I accidentally invented my first card game—with the assistance of my then-eight-year-old son—to explain the core algorithm. (More about that later.)

When it was time to move on from the startup, I found myself in branding and content roles at a handful of creative marketing agencies just outside Washington, DC, supporting clients in the defense and intelligence markets with a few cybersecurity startups on the side. You could say I sort of came full circle and became a marketer for the same nerds I was working with a few years prior.

So, What Now?

Today, I spend my days working with technical founders and leaders, product managers, and marketing teams to identify and nail their market messaging. As a nerd myself, I love working directly with technical people in an organization to draw out gold-nugget messaging elements and put them on display in what I call their first-principles messaging.

I've helped pivot early-stage companies toward human-first messaging, improving their websites to the point where qualified inbound leads increased by 400% in the first year. And I've aligned internal technical teams at multibillion-dollar defense contractors around a bigger corporate vision, something previously considered a big joke.

To do this, I deploy a little bit of what I call "message therapy" (not a typo) to make sure they not only cover the technical "how" details of their story, but also the "so what?," the "why?," and sometimes the "wtf?" elements that really engage customers.

This book is an in-depth look into the philosophies, methods, and frameworks that I've used to pull some of the most hardcore nerds out of their shells until they were world-class communicators and advocates for their own companies. The book is broken into four major parts:

- **Part One**: Focuses on philosophical and scientific background material to help us understand why technical marketing sometimes falls flat to human ears.

- **Part Two**: Presents my philosophy on creating a well-balanced messaging stack.

- **Part Three**: Contains a step-by-step model for executing a successful messaging workshop.

- **Part Four**: Includes a whole bunch of other fun reading and resources that will help to reinforce your messaging. After all, what nerd can resist a little extra-credit homework?

I sincerely hope it all helps your journey into the ranks of the *nerds that talk good*!

PART ONE

The Basics

Remixing the Classics for Modern Messaging

The word "nerd" traditionally refers to a person who is highly intellectual, passionate, or obsessed with a particular subject or field. Many references also go on to include aspects of nerds being perceived as socially awkward or overly focused on niche interests.

It's a definition like a double-edged sword.

We nerds often tend to be very action oriented and tactically focused. Regardless of your preferred topic, I'll bet there's a subject or two in your life on which you could spend hours sharing complex theories, listing interesting facts, or engaging in deep philosophical discussions. From "soup to nuts," as they say.

I'd also wager you've run into situations when the person on the other end of the conversation wasn't quite putting all the puzzle pieces together.

As we'll discuss in this section, we nerds sometimes need to take a step back and establish some fundamentals in order to lay a foundation for higher-complexity conversations. After all, everyone starts somewhere.

This section presents a 101-level exploration of how our brains receive and process information so we can identify why technical messaging fails, and presents what we can learn from some of the world's greatest thinkers to make it work. For clues, we'll look at some theoretical foundations from ancient philosophy, evolutionary biology, and psychology.

Why Bother Talking Good?

For the Skeptical Nerds Out There

"Thoughts are wonderful things, that they can bring two people, so far apart, into harmony and understanding for even a little while."

Ernest "Ernie" Pyle
American journalist and war correspondent

If you've picked up this book, it's likely because you are in one of the following situations or something similar:

- You've been asked to present a technical talk to corporate executives or other nontechnical folk.

- You're an inventor or startup founder who keeps getting prospective customer or funding doors slammed in your face.

- You dread the "so, what do you do?" question at social events or family gatherings.

In each of these situations—and many more—the ability to quickly communicate is often more important than technical prowess. Don't believe me? Think about some of the biggest technical success stories of the past 20 years:

- **Apple Computer**: Rose to be the first trillion-dollar company in 2018, overshadowing technically superior competitors on the back of a charismatic CEO and successful marketing.[4]

- **Tesla**: Despite poor build quality and "quirky" software issues, Tesla Inc. often ranks above Toyota as one of the most valuable automotive companies in the world.[5]

- **Oculus**: Its Quest headset was considered a mediocre competitor in the virtual-reality space until Facebook purchased the technology for $2 billion and incorporated it into its ecosystem.[6]

None of these companies has been the first, best, or only option. But they're the ones that most consumers think of when asked to name a computer company, electric car, or VR headset.[7]

Think about your own experiences. Have you ever looked at some "successful" people and wondered how they got to where they are? Chances are they weren't the best at what they did, but they likely had a certain undefinable "edge" in how they presented or carried themselves.

They did something that made someone around them sit up and pay attention.

---

4   Rob Davies, "Apple Becomes World's First Trillion-Dollar Company," *Guardian* (U.S.), August 2, 2018, https://www.theguardian.com/technology/2018/aug/02/appl e-becomes-worlds-first-trillion-dollar-company.

5   "Tesla Overtakes Toyota to Become World's Most Valuable Carmaker," *BBC*, July 1, 2020, https://www.bbc.com/news/business-53257933.

6   Brian Solomon, "Facebook Buys Oculus, Virtual Reality Gaming Startup, For $2 Billion," *Forbes*, March 25, 2014, https://www.forbes.com/sites/brian-solomon/2014/03/25/facebook-buys-oculus-virtual-reality-gaming-startup-fo r-2-billion/.

7   So much for Zune, Polestar, and HTC Vive.

Paying Attention, in This Economy?

Why is this?

You've probably heard of the so-called "attention economy." Coined by Nobel laureate economist Herbert A. Simon in 1971, the concept revolves around the idea that human attention is a finite resource that can be captured and monetized. He wrote, "A wealth of information creates a poverty of attention."[8]

One significant consequence of the attention economy is the commodification of attention. Just as natural resources like oil and minerals have economic value, so too has human attention become a valuable commodity. Companies and advertisers pay top dollar for our attention as it can directly translate into profits and revenue. This has given rise to various attention-grabbing techniques like clickbait headlines, social media notifications, and targeted advertising.

The attention economy has also had a profound impact on our relationships. In the past, people primarily interacted with each other in person or through traditional forms of media like books, newspapers, and television.

Today, the digital landscape has created countless ways to connect with others, often at the expense of face-to-face interactions. Even our "social" interactions are controlled by platforms designed to keep us engaged and scrolling, often leading to reduced in-person socialization and potentially isolating individuals.

At its core, the attention economy is driven by the recognition that we as humans are constantly shifting our focus between competing needs.

---

[8] Herbert A. Simon, "Designing Organizations for an Information-Rich World," in *Computers, Communications, and the Public Interest*, ed. Martin Greenberger (Johns Hopkins Press, 1971), 38-52.

What Does That Mean for You?

Even when presenting in person to someone, there's a chance that they're subconsciously ticking through a mental to-do list or replaying a recent phone conversation in their head. If you're not the most important, most engaging, most relevant thing happening to them at that moment, you've lost the attention economy.

In fact, research has shown that time and again, people are more likely to invest in or work with people and companies they like over "technically better" options. Plus, they'll often pay a premium for that experience.[9]

This holds true for personal life just as much as it does for professional life. Whether pitching a product or trying to land a job, if you're competing on details alone, the alternative that stands out even a little bit on an emotional level will likely beat you. Emotion drives—and is often required to make—decisions.[10]

The Good News!

Luckily for you and me, it's not difficult to develop that edge. You don't need to become a masterful copywriter, brand expert, or Toastmaster.

Looking for the secret to standing out? It's not "speaking well." You only have to speak as good (or a little good-er) as the next person.

---

[9] A study published in the *Journal of Consumer Research* found that brand loyalty is often driven by emotional bonds, leading consumers to choose familiar brands even when alternatives offer better technical features. This suggests that emotional attachment can outweigh technical considerations in purchasing decisions: Rita Pina and Álvaro Dias, "The Influence of Brand Experiences on Consumer-Based Brand Equity," *Journal of Brand Management* 28 (2020), 99-115, https://doi.org/10.1057/s41262-020-00215-5.

[10] In his book *Descartes' Error*, neuroscientist Antonio Damasio explores his research on individuals with damaged connections between thinking and emotional regions of the brain, revealing that they could analyze choices logically but struggled to decide due to an inability to feel emotions about the options.

Before We Move On

Take a moment to reflect on where you want to improve your communications and who/what you might be comparing yourself to (or want to edge out) by answering these prompts:

> I often feel most challenged when I'm communicating about ...
>
> The person/brand/company that does an excellent job of communicating is ...

This will give us something to set our eyes on as we proceed.

2

The Heart, the Head, and the Gut

Aristotle's Rhetoric for Technical Messaging

"The trouble with market research is that people don't think what they feel, they don't say what they think, and they don't do what they say."

Attributed to David Ogilvy
American advertising pioneer

Let's face it, technical marketing is absurd. There's an overabundance of information and heightened competition for attention. You've got to hook an audience in seconds, deliver the value proposition without confusing them, and consistently build trust to succeed and scale.

We see this in successful consumer marketing all the time. But many technical communicators immediately default to talking about capabilities, features, metrics, and widgets. Our instinct is to shove "all the stuff" at our

9

audience and hope it's what they want.

That's a surefire way to overload your audience (at best) or to just be completely ignored (at worst).

What is today's humble, modern technical marketer to do? Look to the old masters of philosophy!

Picture Aristotle in a hoodie, walking the halls of a tech convention hawking B2B SaaS products.[11] He'd surely be out of place, right? But here's the kicker—his teachings on persuasion are more relevant now than ever.

Figure 1. How I picture Aristotle rolling up at a hacker convention.

---

[11] Business-to-business software-as-a-service, for those of you not up on the alphabet soup jargon of the field.

In the fourth century BCE, this Greek philosopher penned a treatise on persuasion. His *Rhetoric* became a foundational framework of persuasion, offering orators and philosophers a powerful approach for captivating their audience and driving action.[12]

I'm talking about Pathos, Logos, and Ethos, the holy trinity of persuasion. And guess what? They're about to become your best friends in crafting killer technical messages.[13]

- **Pathos (hitting the emotional jackpot)**: Let's face it, tech can be dry. Pathos spices things up. It's all about the feels. Yes, even in B2B, emotions matter. Crafting a good story makes your audience sit up and listen, not just nod and scroll.

- **Logos (because logic never goes out of style)**: Facts, figures, and a clear-cut argument—the bread and butter of tech persuasion. This is a data-driven, logic-laden sword that will cut through the fluff to deliver clear, concise, and compelling reasons why your tech solution is the best.

- **Ethos (more than just a buzzword)**: Ethos isn't just about sounding smart or having the most degrees on the wall. It's about trust. In the tech world, where skepticism runs high, ethos is the golden ticket. It shows an audience that you're not just another false tech geek—rather, you actually know your stuff and have the experience to back it up.

From Aristotle to Anatomy

In a typical technical marketer's career path, classical Greek philosophy is not something that comes up much.

---

[12] Aristotle, *Rhetoric*, trans. W. Rhys Roberts, Internet Classics Archive, accessed January 28, 2025, https://classics.mit.edu/Aristotle/rhetoric.html.

[13] For a great primer on this, check out "Argumentative Essay" from Excelsior Online Writing Lab: https://owl.excelsior.edu/rhetorical-styles/argumentative-essay/argumentative-essay-modes-of-persuasion.

So, I remixed it and made it easier to grok.[14] And who remembers their Greek anyhow? Like a true modern-day philosopher, I prefer to use their symbolic anatomical equivalents—and emoji—the heart, head, and gut.

- **The Heart**: Appeals to the emotions, evoking feelings that resonate deeply with the audience.

- **The Head**: Leverages logic and reasoning, providing evidence and data to support claims.

- **The Gut**: Establishes credibility and trust, demonstrating expertise and reliability.

Viewed through these three internal organs, our old friend Aristotle finds renewed relevance. His principles provide a roadmap for crafting messages that cut through the noise, resonate with prospects, and ultimately drive business growth.

By skillfully targeting different organs at different times, you can craft compelling messages that get attention, get remembered, and get results. Balancing these three modes of persuasion can unlock new opportunities, build stronger customer relationships, and drive your business to new heights.

From Someone Smarter than Me

As Joel Klettke, founder of the marketing company Case Study Buddy and brilliant conversion copywriter, is fond of saying:

"You gain attention with emotion, justify engagement with logic, and win customers with credibility."

I had an opportunity to ask Joel to help me unpack this a little bit on my podcast *Nerds That Talk Good*:

"There's no barrier to entry on claims you can make. You can say anything. But when someone else is saying it, when someone is sticking their neck out for you, when they're saying, 'I have verifiably had an experience and found this to be true,' that's compelling.

"There's a difference between saying 'I will save you time and money,' and

---

[14] First used by Robert A. Heinlein in his 1961 science fiction novel *Stranger in a Strange Land* as a fictional Martian word meaning "to understand intuitively or by empathy, to establish rapport with." Grok is a sort of secret code term known today by old-school computer programmers. As a cultural term, it's a great example of what I term a "Mantra," which I'll get into more detail on in chapter 6.

your customer saying, 'I no longer have to go door to door in my office, delivering checks by hand anymore. It all happens automatically.'

"It's the difference between a lived experience and an empty claim. And customers know that." [15]

So, let's spend just a little time unpacking the practical applications of Aristotle's rhetoric further—empowering you to harness the power of persuasion and achieve remarkable results. Together, we will explore how to leverage pathos, logos, and ethos in various marketing channels, including content creation, social media, email campaigns, and sales or technical presentations.

Figure 2. The heart (not to scale)

Heart: Sparking Emotion to Get Attention

You can't just shove white papers and research at most people and expect them to come around to your way of thinking. Heck, you can't even guarantee they'll read them. You've got to "hook" an audience first and give them a reason to want to listen.

Seizing the heart is the art of appealing to the audience's emotions. Before delivering a technical message, first create empathy and emotional resonance with the audience. This will lead to stronger connections with

---

[15] Joel shared this and more with me on my podcast *Nerds That Talk Good* in episode 004: https://nerdthattalksgood.com/podcast/nttg_004/.

prospects and ultimately more conversions.

Storytelling is a powerful tool to tap into an audience's emotions. When telling a story, a connection is created on a personal level. You can make your listeners feel like they are part of the story and evoke emotions like joy, sadness, anger, or fear.

Vivid imagery can also create emotional connections. With it, you can paint a picture in the audience's mind and make them see, hear, and feel what you are describing. This can create a powerful emotional impact and make messages more memorable.

You can't effectively talk to everyone individually. But you can tailor the message to make the audience feel like you are speaking directly to them. Often, using personal terms—you, your, our—works better than using anonymous third-party references—companies, users, organizations, etc.

This requires putting yourself in your listeners' shoes (ideally using actual customer interviews) to identify information about their interests or pain points. By tailoring a message, you can create a stronger connection and make listeners more likely to act.[16]

Skillful use of pathos lets you engage the heart first, leading to stronger connections with prospects sooner—and more conversions in the long run.

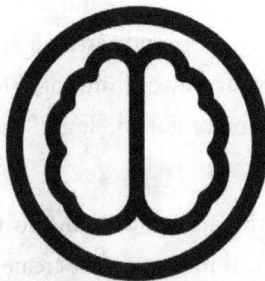

Figure 3. The Head (at least what's in it)

---

[16] We'll take a deeper look at tailoring in chapter 12.

Head: Tickling Curiosity with Logic

Appealing to logic plays a pivotal role in crafting value propositions that resonate deeply with B2B buyers. To effectively leverage logic, customize the value proposition to tickle the intellect of specific buyer personas and alleviate their unique pain points.

Articulating how your solution directly addresses their challenges or needs demonstrates a deep understanding of their business context and shows that you've done your homework and know who they really are.

Highlight unique selling propositions that set you apart from competitors. And, for all that is good in the universe, be unique! If, when walking around a convention floor, you see the same words and phrases on 15 other company banners, find something better to say. Or at least find a different way to say it.

Do some decent research and if players in the market are using the same language, find something you can truly own. Showcase how your product or service offers tangible benefits and competitive advantages that align with the target audience's objectives. Use data-driven insights, statistics, and case studies to support claims and provide empirical evidence of your solution's efficacy.

Present value propositions clearly, using simple language that resonates with the target audience. Avoid confusing jargon and complexities. Ensure that your value proposition is compelling and effectively communicates the value that your solution brings to their business.

It is not necessary to include "all the stuff" on a single page or in a single communication. Instead, evaluate message density and consider whether there are opportunities to break it up into multiple pieces of content. Remember, we are building relationships here, not one-night flings.

Figure 4. The ... Gut?

Gut: Winning Trust with Credibility[17]

The third pillar of Aristotle's rhetoric, ethos, is the art of establishing trust and credibility. This is essential for B2B marketing as buyers are more likely to purchase from a company they trust. There are several ways to build credibility and only a few of them involve numbers. Here are just a few:

- **Metrics**: Yes, cite whatever credible (and provable) metrics there are about your solution. But look to find ways of qualifying them around your value propositions and then weave them into the overall story.

- **External validation**: Look for market research, external statistics, or industry experts who are talking about your problem. Borrow a little trust by using their conversations to make the case for you.

- **Client success stories and testimonials**: It's one thing to talk about yourself. But anything someone else says about you is worth 10 times more. When prospects see that other businesses have benefited from your products or services, they're more likely to believe that you can help them too.

- **Third-party accolades**: Displaying industry certifications and

---

[17] If you're wondering why a burger represents the gut, there are two reasons. First, there isn't a widely accepted stomach emoji in common usage yet. Second, if I had included three organs in the design of my MessageDeck ... ew. So, a burger it is!

awards is another great way to show credibility to potential customers. When they see that industry experts have recognized you, they'll be more confident in your ability to provide high-quality products or services. But beware of pay-to-play awards! These can damage credibility.

Heart, Head, and Gut Across Cultures

The triad of heart, head, and gut goes back way before even Aristotle. It can be found as a discrete trio or as a key part of traditions across cultures and philosophies, uniting emotional, intellectual, and instinctual wisdom into a harmonious whole:

Heart: The Center of Emotions, Love, and Connection

Many traditions see the heart as a bridge between the self and others, as well as a key to spiritual awareness. Whether guiding interpersonal relationships, balancing emotions, or deepening faith, the heart is often seen as the *seat of the soul*.

Philosophical and Cultural Perspectives

- **Taoism** – *Middle Dantian*: The heart center is responsible for emotional harmony and balance.

- **Yoga & Ayurveda** – *Anahata Chakra*: Governs love, compassion, and empathy.

- **Sufism** – *Qalb*: The spiritual heart, the gateway to divine love and awareness.

- **Japanese Philosophy** – *Kokoro*: A unity of heart, spirit, and courage.

- **Huna (Hawaiian Spirituality)** – *Aumakua*: The higher self that provides wisdom and protection.

- **Kabbalah** – *Tiferet*: The balance between judgment and compassion, spiritual beauty.

Head: The Seat of Logic, Insight, and Wisdom

Many traditions consider the head to be the gateway to spiritual enlightenment, rational analysis, and deep insight. Whether through philosophy, meditation, or structured learning, the head is where ideas take shape and knowledge turns into wisdom.

Philosophical and Cultural Perspectives

- **Taoism** – *Upper Dantian*: The center of spiritual clarity and higher thought.[18]

- **Yoga & Ayurveda** – *Sahasrara Chakra*: Connection to higher wisdom and enlightenment.

- **Sufism** – *Aql*: The faculty of rational intelligence and discernment.[19]

- **Japanese Philosophy** – *Shin*: The disciplined mind, clarity, and awareness.

- **Huna (Hawaiian Spirituality)** – *Uhane*: The conscious, thinking mind.

- **Kabbalah** – *Chochmah/Da'at*: Wisdom, knowledge, and intellectual understanding.[20]

---

[18] "Where Is Dantian Located?," Qialance, accessed January 27, 2025, https://qialance.com/where-is-dantian-located/.

[19] "Ruh, Nafs, Qalb and Aql," Hubeali, accessed January 27, 2025, https://hubeali.com/article/ruh-nafs-qalb-and-aql/.

[20] George Robinson, "What Are the Sefirot?" My Jewish Learning, accessed January 27, 2025, https://www.myjewishlearning.com/article/sefirot/.

Gut: The Core of Instinct, Vitality, and Power

Many traditions describe the gut as the foundation of physical and energetic power—where instinct and deep knowing reside. Whether through martial arts, body awareness, or subconscious decision-making, the gut is where action begins.

Philosophical and Cultural Perspectives

- **Taoism** – *Lower Dantian*: The body's core energy source, vital for health and action.

- **Yoga & Ayurveda** – *Manipura Chakra*: The center of willpower, confidence, and personal strength.

- **Sufism** – *Nafs*: The instinctual self, needing discipline and refinement.

- **Japanese Philosophy** – *Hara*: The physical and intuitive center, vital in martial arts.

- **Huna (Hawaiian Spirituality)** – *Unihipili*: The subconscious, primal energy, and survival instincts.

- **Kabbalah** – *Yesod*: The foundation of instinct, action, and connection to the material world.

It's wild how so many traditions nailed this universal balance between what we feel, what we think, and what we just know. Maybe there's a reason why we say, "Listen to your heart," "Use your head," and "Trust your gut." These ancient thinkers were way ahead of the curve!

Persuasion Requires Balance (and Consistency)

There's no "easy button" for technical market communications, and anyone who tells you otherwise is selling something. But my patent-pending messaging framework (Ha! Only half kidding) can help you identify which messaging elements are best suited to hitting the audience where they need it.

We humans, one on one, do pretty well "reading the room" and balancing our communication with a target. But when it comes to developing well-balanced messaging across an organization, things get, well, complex.

People need to hear a particular message approximately seven times before they're ready to take action.[21] And they can spend up to 70% of their time doing their own research before making first contact. This means the messaging that precedes you has to do a lot of heavy lifting. And it needs to be consistent across every channel and campaign.

There's just no room for confusion.

But this book isn't just about tossing around ancient Greek jargon. It's about taking these age-old principles and applying them to today's tech market. We're going to take a deep dive into how to weave pathos, logos, and ethos into a message that stands out, resonates, and converts. For that, we'll need to really understand what's at the root of what we want to say.

Before We Move On:

With the heart, head, and gut in mind, reflect on where you or your team are doing most of your day-to-day communicating.

Is it balanced?

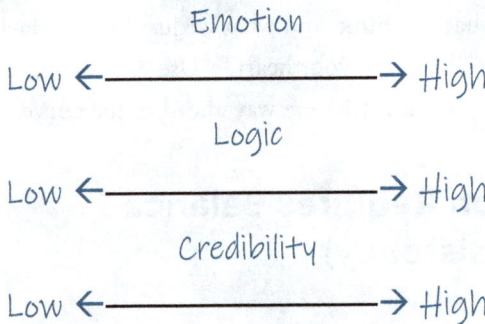

Emotion

Low ←————————→ High

Logic

Low ←————————→ High

Credibility

Low ←————————→ High

---

[21] Fergal Glynn, "Why It Takes Seven to Eight Marketing Touches to Generate a Viable Sales Lead," *The 360 Blog*, April 16, 2015, https://www.salesforce.com/blog/takes-6-8-touches-generate-viable-sales-lead-heres-why-gp/.

3

The Thing That Makes the Thing

Discovering the Essence of Thought

"The great enemy of clear language is insincerity. When there is a gap between one's real and one's declared aims, one turns as it were instinctively to long words and exhausted idioms, like a cuttlefish spurting out ink."

George Orwell
British novelist and poet[22]

꩜

Plato, the great-great-grandaddy of all Western philosophy, spent a lot of time arguing that the *ousia*, or "essence" of something, was both ephemeral and physical in nature.

---

[22] Orwell is either reviled or praised in tech circles, having "predicted" the surveillance state that so many nerds find themselves on one or the other side of. But his 1946 essay "Politics and the English Language" is a must-read for anyone pursuing communications. Find it linked in Additional Reading and References.

Plato's student Aristotle picked up on this topic and expanded on it in his work *Metaphysics*. He called it *to ti ên einai* (τὸ τί ἦν εἶναι)—literally meaning "the what it was to be."[23]

For Plato and Aristotle, essence was both part of and the determining factor of substance. For us, we must first consider the essence of our message before we set about developing it. The intent of your message is its "essence."

There can be a vast difference between what you intend to say and the words used to say it. And sadly, many professionals often get so wrapped around the axle of the words (taglines, headlines, slogans, calls to action, etc.) that the meaning gets muddled or completely forgotten.

Before concerning yourself with all that, lay down a bare-bones understanding of what you want an audience to walk away with after encountering your messaging. Do they need to:

- Have their world rocked and their complacency disabused?

- Be invited into a new era of business?

- Be comforted by an ally?

These are just examples of directional essence statements. You may, and likely will, reconsider these as you get deeper into message discovery. But having a few to start with is very handy for setting a compass direction moving forward.

Clarity vs. Focus

You can think about the dual nature of messaging as similar to the relationship between clarity and focus.

These concepts—which have distinct meanings—are often used in various contexts, including photography, writing, and cognitive processes.

---

23   For a layperson's primer on Aristotle's *Metaphysics*, check out the Stanford Encyclopedia of Philosophy: https://plato.stanford.edu/entries/aristotle-metaphysics/.

Clarity

The quality of being clear, easily seen, or heard.

Consider an object on a table in front of you. It could be an apple, a deck of playing cards, or another simple thing. Without any distortion or anything getting in the way, what you might see is the item in its purest form. Its "essence."

If you were to put on a pair of glasses (I'm partial to the term "specs" myself) with perfectly clear lenses, you'd see the object more or less as it is, or as it was intended.[24] This lens represents clarity in marketing communication. Just as a clear lens allows you to see an image without distortion or blurriness, clarity in messaging ensures that the audience can understand the marketing without confusion.

A smudge or a scratch on the lens represents unclear communication, which distorts the viewer's understanding, like how jargon or a convoluted message can confuse or mislead a customer.

Clarity refers to the quality of being clear and understandable. It's about the sharpness of the expression, whether in writing, speech, or visual representation. It ensures that the message or image is conveyed in a way that is easy to understand and leaves little room for confusion or misinterpretation.

In a photographic or visual context, clarity refers to how sharp and distinct the details in an image are. A photo with high clarity will be crisp and textures will be well-defined.

So, essence statements provide clarity. But you may not want a stark and crisp message. That can be boring. You may want to spice things up by "projecting" the image onto an audience with a funky, more personalized lens. This is where focus comes in.

---

[24] No lens is 100% perfect. Anything between you and the object would technically interfere. And I'm also assuming your eyesight is good. But go with me for the metaphor here.

Focus

A center of activity, attraction, or attention.

In photography, focus is about the specific part of the image that is sharp. A camera lens can be focused on a particular subject, making it sharp, while other parts of the image might be blurred by controlling how much light enters through the lens. This is called the "f-stop;" determining which part of the image draws the viewer's attention.[25]

If clarity in messaging is about ensuring that it's easily comprehensible and detailed, focus is about where attention is directed and making it relevant to the channel and audience. It's about channeling attention or effort to a specific point or task, concentrating and homing in on a particular aspect while ignoring distractions.

Not to get all "linear communication theory" on you, but in communications, intent comes first. Therefore, clarity comes first. And it's a funny coincidence that the word "clarity" came into use nearly 300 years before "focus."[26]

If you don't take the time to very deliberately identify (and capture) core meanings and takeaways before embarking on execution, chances are you risk going to market with a confusing message. And if you are on a team of more than two, you risk misalignment within the organization, which will result in disjointed and inconsistent messages across the full campaign and content landscape.

As this is not a "marketing" book, most of my attention is on clarity.

---

[25] Nicole Morrison, "Learn About F-Stop Photography and What It Does," Adobe, accessed January 28, 2025, https://www.adobe.com/creativecloud/photography/discover/f-stop.html.

[26] Etymologists mark "clarity" as coming into use around 1380, while "focus" didn't make its debut until the mid-1600s. *Oxford English Dictionary*, "clarity," accessed January 30, 2025, https://www.oed.com/dictionary/clarity_n; *Oxford English Dictionary*, "focus," accessed January 30, 2025, https://www.oed.com/dictionary/focus_n.

Which is not to say we won't put our focus (heh!) on focus later.

But first, message principles need to be established before turning them into the taglines and headlines that we all love so much.

4

Your Buyer Is a Caveman

Using Modern Psychology for Archaic Neurology

"Our modern skulls house a Stone Age mind."

Leda Cosmides and John Tooby
Pioneers in evolutionary psychology

👓

You'll often hear marketing and communications gurus chant the phrase *know your audience* as the key to tailoring a message. While that's very important, knowing your own biases is equally important—if not more so.

As practitioners very close to our tech day in and day out, it's easy to forget that not everyone is as quick to see "obvious" patterns as we are. You can't expect someone to come to the same conclusions as you, even when presented with the same information.

Ant Tunnels and Cracker Crumbs

As I mentioned earlier, between my time as a federal communications manager and marketing strategist I joined an early-stage cybersecurity company that was founded by the hiring manager who had brought me to DHS. Based on his PhD thesis, he had created a model for developing a self-defending network based on the swarming patterns of eusocial insects, like ants and bees.[27]

He invited me to be his director of communications and marketing, which I excitedly accepted. We adopted the metaphor of ants to explain our "secret sauce." In fact, we went a little overboard with the metaphor. We "swarmed" conferences wearing t-shirts from the Marvel *Ant-Man* franchise and incorporated ants into every piece of our marketing material. To this day, I still have a bag of small plastic ants in my office, because … reasons.

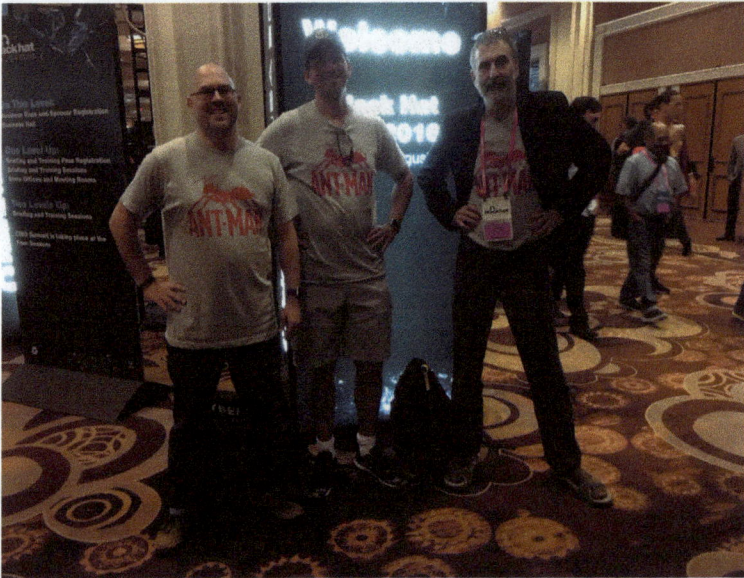

Figure 5. The "Ant-Men" at the 2018 BlackHat Conference

---

[27] Yes, it was as nerdy and fascinating as it sounds. A link to Earl's thesis is in Additional Reading and References (along with some other geeky reading).

We tried several ways to describe the algorithm to prospects and investors. Our lead developer, Michael, and I had a perpetual disagreement over whether we should describe the ant colony optimization as how ants "foraged for food" or "built their tunnels."

Michael would wax mathematical regarding how the algorithm was more accurate about building the underlying structures of their defense mechanisms.

One day, I reminded him that the average person had probably never seen or given much thought to what ant tunnels looked like, because they're buried in the ground. But almost everybody had dealt with ants crawling from crumb to crumb in their kitchen.

"Maybe it's not *technically* the most accurate," I concluded. "But is it correct *enough* to get the point across without introducing more questions so we can get someone to the next stage in the conversation?"

"*Technically* speaking, an ant colony optimization algorithm *is* a probabilistic technique for solving computational problems which *can* be reduced to finding good paths through graphs based on pheromone concentration," Michael responded. (When we reached this point in the conversation, I knew I had gotten close enough.)

In the end, neither approach even mattered because we ultimately discovered that trying to introduce ants in the first place proved to be counterproductive. It was a nice but unnecessary technical detail that meant starting each pitch with a biology lesson, piling on additional information that was ultimately irrelevant to the needs of a chief information officer.

Lesson Learned: Beware of Biases

In 1999, Warner Bros. released a movie that would forever change the style and aesthetics of computer culture. *The Matrix* was beloved by an entire generation of hackers and kung-fu aficionados alike.

Without too much exposition,[28] intelligent machines have enslaved humanity—plugging everyone into a collective virtual reality called the "Matrix." A small band of freedom fighters have escaped into the real world and battle for the future of humanity. From the outside, however, the Matrix can only be observed by watching raw code scroll by on computer monitors.

In a scene halfway through the film, the protagonist Neo walks into a command center where the computer operator Cypher is sitting in front of a bank of screens:

> Neo: Is that ...?
>
> Cypher: The Matrix? [nods] Yeah.
>
> Neo: Do you always look at it encoded?
>
> Cypher: Well, you have to. The image translators work for the construct program. But there's way too much information to decode the Matrix. You get used to it. I ... I don't even see the code. All I see is blonde, brunette, redhead. Hey, you uh ... want a drink?[29]

I Don't Even See the Code

It's a seemingly insignificant scene; this conversation takes less than a minute in total. But Cypher's "I don't even see the code" tells you a great deal about what many call *the curse of expertise*. This is a cognitive bias that occurs when an individual communicating with others assumes that the person they are talking to has the same information, inferring that everyone shares the same background and understanding. Some also call this the curse of knowledge.

Many technical practitioners are so close to their subject of expertise, able to make conclusions or interpretations so easily, that they forget that

---

28   For real, though. If you haven't seen *The Matrix*, put this book down, pop some popcorn, and go watch it!

29   *The Matrix*, directed by Lana and Lilly Wachowski (Warner Brothers, 1999).

not everyone around them is on the same level.

But, as we'll see, even if an audience can understand on the same level as you, it doesn't mean you should make them do so.

The Curse of Knowledge

It's worth mentioning that Cypher eventually betrays humanity and strikes a deal with the machines to have his memory wiped and inserted back into the Matrix.

"I know this steak doesn't exist," he says, slicing into a rare cut of beef in a restaurant simulation. "I know that when I put it in my mouth, the Matrix is telling my brain that it is juicy and delicious. After nine years, you know what I realize? Ignorance is bliss."

I suppose there is a risk to knowing too much about a subject after all.

What's This About the Caveman?

The title of this chapter is not meant to be inflammatory (or gender-exclusive). It's sympathetic. The brain is a wonderful computer, capable of anything you throw at it. Or is it?

Psychology Today eloquently recounts the processing power of the brain on their website:

> Your brain is a three-pound universe that processes 70,000 thoughts each day using 100 billion neurons that connect at more than 500 trillion points through synapses with signals that travel 300 miles/hour.[30]

However, despite how complex and wonderful our hardware (or is it wetware?) is, when it comes to software, we are still operating on a 100,000-year-old beta release that has several real-world bottlenecks.

If you pay close attention during sales presentations, demos, or even

---

[30] Jeffrey Bernstein, "The Most Overlooked Strategy for Success," *Psychology Today*, last updated October 22, 2023, https://www.psychologytoday.com/us/blog/liking-the-child-you-love/202310/the-most-overlooked-strategy-for-success.

watch web traffic, you can identify when an audience starts to hit their limit. I call it the "Blank Stare" moment.

It's the point where you're either overwhelming the audience with too many data points or underwhelming them emotionally and they check out.

How to avoid this?

It's not glitzier marketing or shoving more "stuff" at them. Sometimes, it's less.

The Rule of Three

Ever noticed that people have an almost irresistible attraction to items that come in threes?

The smart folks at the University of Oregon have figured out that our brains can only handle about four thoughts at once. This limitation seems to be about the hardware.[31]

The significance of the number three in human thought, often encapsulated in the "rule of three," relates to cognitive and psychological patterns observed across various contexts.

- **Memory and information processing**: Grouping information into threes can make it more manageable and memorable because it is the smallest number of items necessary for our brains to apply pattern recognition. Humans tend to find it easier to grasp and remember information in chunks of three. This is supported by psychological research on working memory, which suggests that people can hold about three to four items in their working memory at one time.[32]

---

[31] Edward Awh, Brian Barton, and Edward K. Vogel, "Visual Working Memory Represents a Fixed Number of Items Regardless of Complexity," *Psychological Science* 18, no. 7 (2007): 622–28, https://doi.org/10.1111/j.1467-9280.2007.01949.x.

[32] Earl K. Miller and Timothy J. Buschman, "Working Memory Capacity: Limits on the Bandwidth of Cognition," *Daedalus* 144, no. 1 (2015): 112–22, https://doi.org/10.1162/DAED_a_00320.

- **Communication and rhetoric**: The rule of three is a powerful rhetorical device used throughout history in speeches, writing, and advertising. Phrases or ideas presented in threes are more persuasive and satisfying to an audience. This pattern can be seen in famous examples like the American Declaration of Independence's "Life, Liberty, and the pursuit of Happiness" or Bill Murray's line "We came, we saw, we kicked its ass!" from the movie *Ghostbusters*.[33]

- **Narrative structure**: In storytelling and other forms of narrative, the number three is often used to structure plot and character development. Classic story arcs might involve three acts (beginning, middle, end) or three main characters to enhance balance and resolution in the narrative.

Take It Easy

Some years ago, ESPN published an often-challenged article claiming that champion chess players can burn up to 6,000 calories a day while seated and concentrating on playing chess.[34] While I can't say for sure that I've ever broken out in a sweat when confronted with a hefty mental task, I think we can all relate to flopping down onto the couch at the end of a particularly brain-heavy workday. So, why subject your audience to any more cognitive load than necessary?

Humans have a natural inclination toward decisions that require a lower cognitive load. Why? It's a tendency deeply rooted in our evolutionary past. This preference can be traced back to the "caveman brain," or more formally, the limbic system, which is responsible for our instinctive behaviors and emotions.

The limbic system—including structures like the amygdala and

---

[33] With apologies to Julius Caesar's "Veni, Vidi, Vici" (I came, I saw, I conquered).

[34] Aishwarya Kumar, "The Grandmaster Diet: How To Lose Weight While Barely Moving," ESPN, April 27, 2020, https://www.espn.com/espn/story/_/id/27593253/why-grandmasters-magnus-carlsen-fabiano-caruana-lose-weight-playing-chess.

hippocampus—is an evolutionarily ancient part of the human brain that's geared toward survival. It's always on the lookout for threats and rewards, driving us to make quick, energy-efficient decisions. This is because, in our prehistoric past, taking too long to decide could mean the difference between escape or becoming dinner for a saber-toothed tiger. Quick decision-making conserved energy and allowed our ancestors to react swiftly to dangers and opportunities.

As Simple as Ordering a Coffee

Imagine walking into a café craving a simple cup of coffee only to be confronted with a menu longer than your arm with each item containing a paragraph's worth of technical data: country or origin, acidity levels, serving temperature, caffeine content, and so on.

Suddenly, satisfying that craving turns into a chore.

The last thing you want to do is burden an audience and make them regret clicking on your website or taking an introductory demo.

Sadly, we do this all the time as technical marketers. Day in and day out, navigating a world brimming with data, options, and constant negotiations, we often don't realize the mental toll it takes on our ability to make decisions. By presenting an audience with a barrage of mental tasks, we unwittingly pass on this cognitive load, turning what should be a delight into a burden.

It's not just about being considerate—it's about being strategic. There's science to back me up here. Less is often more. Cutting through the clutter can offer clarity instead of confusion.

Success in modern technical sales, marketing, and really any persuasion comes down to cutting cognitive burden.

You might be thinking, "But, Joel, I'm talking about highly technical things. There is a lot of very important detail I need to put in front of my audience to get them to understand what I'm talking about."

Yes. But each detail presents the audience with a choice, which requires an extra bit of their mental RAM. Don't believe me? Let's meet our two brains.

Your Two Brains

The human brain has different systems that help us pay attention to tasks and our environment. Two key networks involved in attention are the dorsal attention network (DAN) and the ventral attention network (VAN).

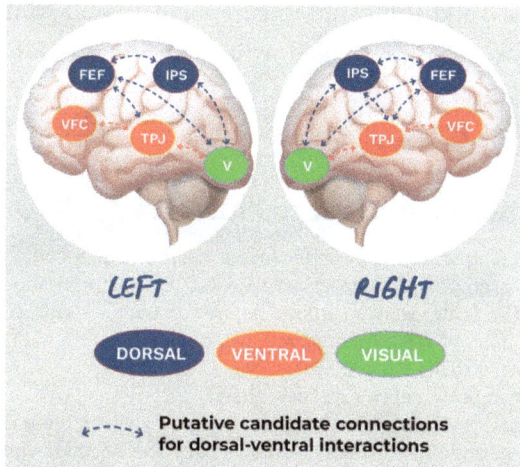

Figure 6. Meet your two brains. Simone Vossel, Joy J. Geng, and Gereon R. Fink, "Dorsal and Ventral Attention Systems," Neuroscientist 20, no. 2 (2014): 150–59, https://doi.org/10.1177/1073858413494269 (CC BY 3.0).

Let's break them down in lay terms:

- **Dorsal attention network (DAN)**: Think of this as the brain's director. It's like a manager who focuses on what is important and keeps you concentrated on the task at hand. When intentionally trying to pay attention, like studying for an exam or driving through heavy traffic, the dorsal network is at work. It's goal-directed and helps you maintain focus despite distractions.

- **Ventral attention network (VAN):** On the other hand, the VAN is more like your brain's alert system. Imagine reading a book in a quiet room; suddenly, you hear a loud noise. It's the VAN that makes you snap your head up to see what's going on. It's responsible for detecting unexpected events or stimuli, especially when something new or surprising happens that might be important. It's not about focusing on a task; it's about being ready to shift attention to something else if necessary.

So, the dorsal network is about voluntary focus, and the ventral network is about involuntary attention shifts. They work together to help you navigate a world full of information and stimuli while also letting you concentrate when needed and redirecting attention when something important or unusual occurs.

A Thought Experiment to Illustrate

Imagine being at a fancy dinner in the ballroom of a conference center. Without any prompting, you're asked to enter the ballroom and expected to spend 10 to 15 minutes walking around before coming back out.

After this time, you're presented with two questions:

1. How many chairs did you see?
2. How many emergency exits were there?

Chances are, your brain didn't register how many chairs there were because it's irrelevant information. After all, you only have one backside and can only sit in one chair at a time. But I'll bet you could provide the number of exits within a reasonable margin of error.

Why?

Survival.

What's the Difference Between Chairs and Exits?

The difference is the vigilant VAN. That primitive self-preservation part of your brain is constantly taking in information and making decisions about whether it's relevant to preserving your life and the human species.

What happens when we begin overloading these attention networks with even more superfluous information? The brain starts "dropping packets."[35]

The Paradox of Choice

In terms of neuroscience, studies have shown that cognitive load can inhibit the brain's decision-making processes. When faced with too many choices, the prefrontal cortex—which is responsible for complex behaviors such as planning and decision making—can become overwhelmed. This leads to a decrease in decision-making efficiency and an increase in stress and anxiety, even if we're not consciously aware of it.

Furthermore, research into decision making also touches on the concept of decision fatigue.[36] The more choices we have to make, the more depleted our cognitive resources become, leading to poorer quality decisions as the day progresses. This is why simpler choices, or the default "no-brainer" options, become more appealing—they preserve our cognitive resources.

Books like *Thinking, Fast and Slow* by Daniel Kahneman delve into the dual-process theory of the brain, which describes the interplay between the fast, instinctual, and emotional system (akin to our cavebrain) and the slow, deliberate, and logical system (the more evolved aspects of the brain involved in complex cognition).[37] These systems compete and collaborate in the decision-making process, with the primitive brain often taking the lead in situations that require low cognitive load or quick responses.

The human tendency to opt for decisions that require less thinking is a vestige of our need for cognitive efficiency and energy conservation—the result of brain design shaped by millions of years of evolution.

---

[35] Packet loss is a networking term measured as a percentage of packets lost with respect to packets sent. There's always an acceptable level. A little bit might be okay. But too much means your Netflix keeps stalling and a poor quality of experience (QOE).

[36] [37] In one study, shoppers presented with 24 jam varieties were less likely to make a purchase than those who saw only six varieties, indicating that too many choices can lead to mental fatigue and choice paralysis. Barry Schwartz, "More Isn't Always Better," *Harvard Business Review*, June 2006, https://hbr.org/2006/06/more-isnt-always-better.

[37] Daniel Kahneman, *Thinking, Fast and Slow* (Farrar, Straus and Giroux, 2013).

Can We "Hack" the Brain?

Master brand strategist and founder of the Brand Master Academy, Stephen Houraghan, has a lot to say about caveman brain. In one of my favorites of his social media posts, he squarely identifies several "tricks" that leverage what we know about how our brain operates. It operates on two basic premises.

1. The human brain is a complex organ that controls your every decision.

2. But the decision-making mind is a primitive and simplistic mechanism.

In his post, Houraghan shared five "primitive brain hacks":

1. **Sensuality is seductive**: Who doesn't love a sensory experience? Leverage the power of sight, sound, and smell to create a brand experience that your audience won't forget.

2. **Value is perceived**: It's not just about what you offer, but how you communicate it. Use strategic messaging to shape your audience's perception of your brand and increase its perceived value.

3. **Focus on small steps**: Taking the first step can be daunting. Make it easy for your audience by breaking down your brand journey into micro-commitments they can easily tackle.

4. **Opportunity knocks once**: The primitive mind is hardwired to avoid missed opportunities. Create a sense of urgency with your brand messaging to encourage your audience to take action before it's too late.

5. **Like minds connect**: Empathy and understanding are crucial to building strong connections with your audience. Speak to their pain points and desires with a human touch and watch your brand loyalty grow.

I don't know about you, but to me, it sure sounds like a lot of emotion and credibility are involved—and not much logic.[38]

When I asked Houraghan why these hacks work so well, he summed it all up in one concept—simplification:

> For all the complexity that our consciousness and advanced neo-cortex contribute," he said, "it's our primitive brain that runs the subconscious program beneath the surface. When we strip the complexity back, we are simple beings with simple problems trying to achieve simple objectives. Looking at it through this lens, it becomes obvious. The role of branding is about simplification.

So, keep it simple, smarty-pants!

Respecting the Cavebrain

So, what to do with all this information I've now inadvertently overloaded you with?

Remember that every word added to your homepage or collateral and every phrase that comes out of your mouth is something an audience's collective brain needs to do something with.

At best, they had better be advancing your objective (and you'd better know what that objective is) at every stage. At a minimum, they had better not be introducing doubt or slowing down that next "yes!" decision.

Your best path is making very deliberate decisions about what's in and what's out of the messaging, getting your team on board with it (the whole team), and being consistent with go-to-market activities.

---

[38] Check out Stephen's post at LinkedIn: https://www.linkedin.com/posts/stephe n-houraghan_5-primitive-mind-hacks-activity-7047540333403906049-aw9g/. And be sure to give his Brand Master Academy program a try!

You *can* control that blank stare moment.

You just need a plan, which we'll begin building together in Part Two. First, however, we need to figure out what people need.

5

First-Principles Messaging

Abraham Maslow's Hierarchy of Needs for Audience Focus

*"Belief in oneself and knowing who you are, I mean, that's
the foundation for everything great."*

Jay Z
American rapper and entrepreneur

👓

In 1943, American psychologist Abraham Maslow published "A Theory of Human Motivation" in the journal *Psychological Review*. In it, he proposed a psychological theory that categorizes human needs into a five-level pyramid often used for understanding human motivation, personal development, and psychological health.[39]

---

[39] Abraham Maslow, "A Theory of Human Evolution," *Psychological Review* 50, no. 4 (1943): 370-96, https://doi.org/10.1037/h0054346.

His "pyramid of needs" theory is depicted with the more fundamental needs at the base and the more esoteric ones at the top.

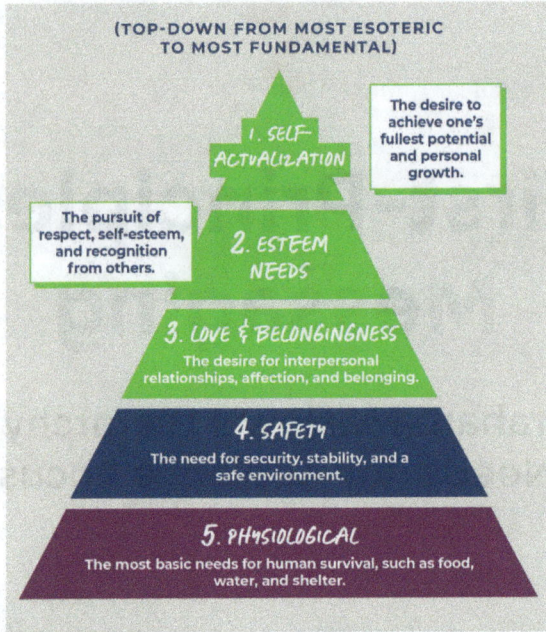

(TOP-DOWN FROM MOST ESOTERIC TO MOST FUNDAMENTAL)

1. SELF-ACTUALIZATION
The desire to achieve one's fullest potential and personal growth.

2. ESTEEM NEEDS
The pursuit of respect, self-esteem, and recognition from others.

3. LOVE & BELONGINGNESS
The desire for interpersonal relationships, affection, and belonging.

4. SAFETY
The need for security, stability, and a safe environment.

5. PHYSIOLOGICAL
The most basic needs for human survival, such as food, water, and shelter.

Figure 7: Overview of Maslow's hierarchy (top-down from most esoteric to most fundamental)

Interestingly, while Maslow is credited with the pyramid concept, his original work does not represent it visually. Regardless, this concept of a pyramid hierarchy has had a significant impact in various fields outside of psychology, such as education, business, and marketing—becoming a key visual in countless motivational and marketing slides since.

The key to Maslow's Hierarchy of Needs is the concept that humans need to meet fundamental needs before they can fully access or fulfill "upper" ones. It's right there in the name "hierarchy" after all. In his conclusion, Maslow wrote:

> These basic goals are related to each other, being arranged in a hierarchy of prepotency. This means that the

most prepotent goal will monopolize consciousness and will tend of itself to organize the recruitment of the various capacities of the organism. The less prepotent needs are ... minimized, even forgotten or denied. But when a need is fairly well satisfied, the next prepotent ('higher') need emerges, in turn to dominate the conscious life and to serve as the center of organization of behavior, since gratified needs are not active motivators.[40]

To quote C.S. Lewis, "When first things are put first, second things are not suppressed but increased."[41] You can't get to the top if you don't first look to the basics. It's all co-dependent.

Digging Deeper

It's worth noting that there is debate about whether Maslow originated the concept of a needs hierarchy after all.[42]

Maslow spent time in the summer of 1938 at the Blackfoot Reserve in Alberta, Canada. During this time, he observed the community and social structures. Some argue that Maslow's observations of Blackfoot society influenced his development of the Hierarchy of Needs, particularly the concepts of community and self-actualization, though no references to their beliefs appear in his work on the hierarchy.

The Blackfoot concept of well-being is not strictly hierarchical but rather interconnected, focusing on the balance between the individual, the community, and the natural world. Their strong sense of community and the importance of social bonds likely influenced Maslow's inclusion of love and belonging as fundamental human needs. The holistic view of well-being, where physical, emotional, social, and spiritual needs are interconnected, may have contributed to Maslow's idea of self-actualization.

He seems to have lost the plot a little bit. Whereas the Blackfoot belief system seems to ask, "How do we become a more actualized society?" Maslow's theory is more focused on "How can I become a better me?"

Personally, I find the Blackfoot belief system to be more appealing and always feel obligated to give credit where credit is due. But the Maslow model is useful to our present endeavor. So, we'll use it.

---

[40] Maslow, "Theory of Human Evolution."

[41] C. S. Lewis to Mrs. Johnson, November 8, 1952, in *The Collected Letters of C. S. Lewis, Volume III* (HarperCollins, 2007).

[42] For more on this, check out Scott Barry Kaufman, "Who Created Maslow's Iconic Pyramid?," *Scientific American*, April 23, 2019, https://www.scientificamerican.com/blog/beautiful-minds/who-created-maslows-iconic-pyramid/.

Applying a Staged Approach to the Hierarchy

Another interpretation of the hierarchy is that people are more open and susceptible to different needs at different times in their development.[43]

For example, a child is more likely to need more physiological, safety, and security support than an adult pursuing romantic and self-esteem-building activities.

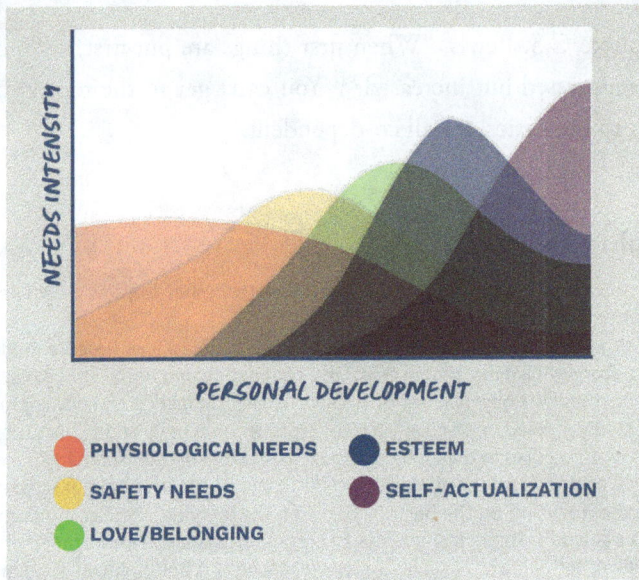

Figure 8. Maslow's needs along dynamic personal development.. David Krech, Richard S. Crutchfield, and Egerton L. Ballachey, Individual in Society: A Textbook of Social Psychology (McGraw-Hill, 1962).

If we "remix" this classic idea into something tailor-made for the world of technical messaging and marketing, we're not just talking basic needs and self-actualization for individuals; we're translating this into a language that resonates with businesses, tech geeks, and yes, even those hard-to-impress C-suite execs.

---

43 David Krech, Richard S. Crutchfield, and Egerton L. Ballachey, *Individual in Society: A Textbook of Social Psychology* (McGraw-Hill, 1962), 77.

By formalizing our framework, we have a mechanism to address the fundamental "what" and "how" of the tech, right up to the "why" that gets everyone excited. Let's dive into this, shall we?

PART TWO

The Building Blocks

Another Freakin' Framework?

You probably feel like you need another framework just about as much as you need another hole in your head. And you're probably right. But stick with me.

Everybody has their own "special sauce" model for looking at the world. And there are many more in-depth marketing frameworks. I'm absolutely not saying that what follows is the be-all and end-all. But it is one useful way of breaking down messaging into manageable chunks that you can use for everything from daily conversations to full-blown presentations.

So don't think of this as a framework. Think of it as a glimpse into the mind of a recovering brand nerd and marketing strategist. It's the structure and system that I needed when I was communicating on behalf of up to a dozen organizations at the same time.

The best way to keep from looking, sounding (and sometimes smelling) like everyone else is to identify everything you might want to say, compare it to the state of the marketplace, and make decisions based on what you *should* say to stand out, be memorable, and build credibility.

And that's the point.

6

From Table Stakes to Taglines

Or, How I Learned to Stop Worrying and Embrace the Conjoined Triangle of Success

"All models are wrong, some are useful."

George Box
British statistician

If experience has taught me anything, shoving all the data at an audience all at once rarely results in a yes. Remember, you can almost see the attention drain from their eyes as their cavebrains overload.

So, how do we make deliberate choices about what to put into messages and when to put them in front of an audience?

Building a modular set of first-principles messaging points that, in combination, strike the right balance of information and inspiration and grab an audience where they are in the buying cycle requires creating a system. Luckily, nerds love systems![44]

I'm not saying this is the be-all and end-all for messaging and communications. But it's a place to start, one that I've made as simple as possible to be accessible to marketers and non-marketers alike.

Similar to the Maslow-inspired popular pyramid depiction, our triangle is structured from bottom to top with more intellectually dense, low-emotion concepts at the bottom and lower-density, higher-emotional concepts at the top.

Meet the Messaging Pyramid

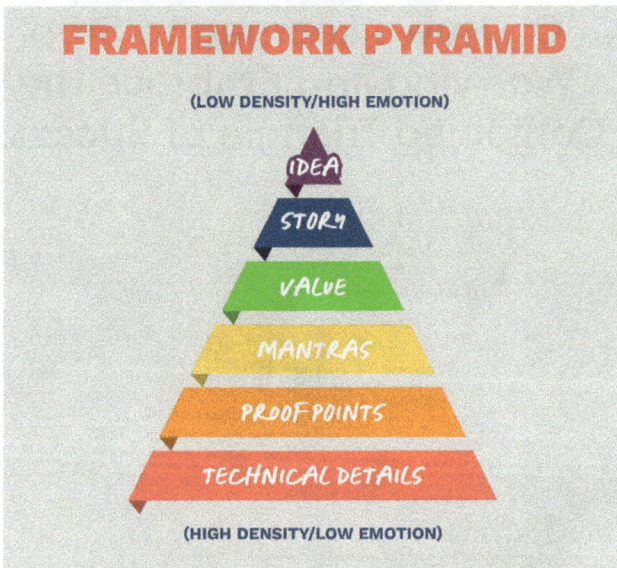

Figure 9. Fancy, fancy framework pyramid

Unlike the Maslow pyramid, the more important concepts sit at the top. This is because far fewer Big Idea and Story elements are needed to hook someone than Proof Points and Technical Details. (Again, Big Ideas are

_____
44   Remember, I can say that because I am one.

stronger than details.)

It's our job as technical communicators to take an audience on a journey from the top of the mountain to the base, as it were.

The Layers

Each layer serves a different need of the audience. Here's a quick rundown of the levels using a few examples from my own messaging:

1. **Ideas**: The big, thematic concepts that should permeate your entire brand or messaging.

    Purpose: Represent the "big why" and the most important takeaway for the audience after the first encounter. Engage emotionally from the start to retain attention.

    Example: *"It pays to be a nerd that talks good."*

2. **Story**: The narrative that connects with the day-to-day experiences of an audience.

    Purpose: Demonstrate context and connect on a human level. Share what makes your organization tick, moving from heart feelings to gut feelings by weaving in logical arguments. Or begin by showing how you fit into the audience's experience.

    Example 1: *"When I got to the government and they realized I could communicate technical concepts clearly, they gave me an incredible opportunity that changed my life."*

    Example 2: *"My experience with startups is that they always want to lead with their special sauce, which can sometimes be a stumbling block for their audience. I found it's much better to lead with an audience's emotional experience."*

3. **Value**: Clear, consistent articulations of the benefits and value you offer to the audience.

    Purpose: Address the audience's needs and answer their "What's in it for me?" question.

Example: *"If you learn to talk good, you'll get more blank checks and fewer blank stares."*

4. **Mantras**: Phrases and concepts that reflect the core beliefs of your organization or the audience.

   Purpose: Serve as genuine statements of culture and truth, going beyond typical marketing slogans.

   Example 1: *"Complex does not have to be confusing."*

   Example 2: *"Get noticed. Get remembered. Get results."*

5. **Proof Points**: Evidence that builds credibility and trust with the audience.

   Purpose: Answers the "Why should I trust you?" question through hard and soft examples, social proofs, and external validations.

   Example 1: *"Thanks, Joel! I believe 'something' is working because customers are flocking in!"*[45]

   Example 2: *"I streamlined a client's list of fourteen features down to just three super categories, which made things much easier on their audience, resulting in more sales leads."*

6. **Technicals**: Detailed information about your technology, solution, or data.

   Purpose: Provide comprehensive technical details in a structured manner, ensuring they are readily accessible and integrated with other messaging levels.

   Example: *"The MessageSpecs method is based on ancient philosophy and modern neuropsychology."*

---

[45] This is from an actual early client of mine! There's nothing better than getting feedback like this and being able to share it.

What to Include When?

Remember that an audience needs different things at different times. American advertising pioneer E. St. Elmo Lewis specifically called this out in his three chief copywriting principles (emphasis added):[46]

> The mission of an advertisement is to **attract a reader**, so that he will look at the advertisement and start to read it; **then to interest him**, so that he will continue to read it; **then to convince him**, so that when he has read it he will believe it. If an advertisement contains these three qualities of success, it is a successful advertisement.[47]

Seems pretty simple, right? It can be. Sadly, many technical organizations and companies seem to overcomplicate this flow. Marketing operations specialists have even expanded this model into complex webs of interactions they like to call "The Marketing Funnel."

You don't have to go so far. Right now, it's enough to understand that there's a series of typical touchpoints your audience needs to step through for a full experience and understanding of your offer.

---

[46] I couldn't have said this better myself. For some additional reading recommendations from Lewis, see Additional Reading in the Appendix.

[47] Elias St. Elmo Lewis, "Catch-Line and Argument," *The Book-Keeper* 15 (1903): 124.

Before We Move On:

Take a moment to reflect on the order in which you typically present information.

Are you delivering top of pyramid stuff first and leading your audience to the deeper, technical goodies? Or are you trying to deliver all the data first and build up to a compelling conclusion?

7

Messages That Matter

Reimagining the Marketing Funnel as a Message Map

"Does your content lead readers on a journey, or does it merely stuff them as leads into a pipeline?"

Ann Handley
Digital marketing leader and author of *Everybody Writes*

👓

One of the things marketers get right is the concept of "marketing funnels." At its core, the concept of a funnel is simple. A marketing funnel is like a path or journey of content that businesses create to guide people from being curious about their product to becoming loyal customers. It's called a "funnel" because it starts wide, with lots of people at the top, and narrows down as only some of those people take the steps to buy.

But, as in most professions with a lot of smart people in it, marketers tend to overcomplicate things. You don't have to fall into that trap when you're

55

developing your messaging. But you can start to adopt some of the concepts to make it easier to build a marketing funnel when you need to later.[48]

Marketing funnels have become intricate webs of activities to measure, brimming with click-through rates and conversion metrics. It's easy to lose sight of the customer by often focusing on tactics or your own agenda.

Ann Handley's incisive quote above reminds us that a successful funnel is not just about moving numbers through a process; it's about crafting a meaningful path for your audience. A marketing funnel should do more than collect leads—it should build a relationship with and guide potential customers with care, empathy, and relevance.

In this chapter, we'll explore how to design messaging for funnels that feel less like assembly lines and more like well-lit paths to mutual understanding and trust. From sparking initial curiosity to solidifying long-term commitment, you'll learn how to align every stage of your messaging with your audience's needs—and create experiences that truly resonate. And you'll do it without marketing fluff.

What's interesting (and nearly accidental) about both the structure and the order of the Foundational Messaging Pyramid is that it roughly aligns with both our "Heart, Head, Gut" objectives and the typical "marketing funnel" used by many marketers.

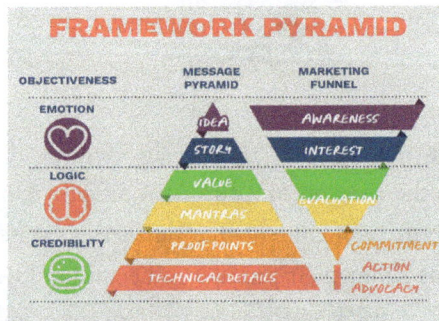

Figure 10. Rough alignment of Aristotelian rhetoric, message pyramid, and marketing funnel

---

[48] Or even better, hand your messaging off to a marketing partner to do it for you.

It's not a *perfect* alignment, though. Logic and Proof Points can be sneaky by overlapping or swapping positions, depending on the audience. But it largely fits.

Messaging Needs at Different Stages

Another way to look at the staged approach is to consider the varying importance of each message element as an individual progresses through their audience journey. If you know where your audience is in their relationship relative to you and you know which message balance works best at that stage, you can more easily develop communications that scratch the right itch at the right time.

This requires breaking up the audience into different categories, depending on where they are in relation to their exposure to the problem, the options out there, and your solution in particular. There are many different "audience journey" stages. But here's a rough explanation of a general progression.

- **Unaware**: At this stage, potential customers are not aware of your product or service. They might not even recognize the problem that your product might solve.

- **Aware**: Potential customers become aware that they have a problem. They may have encountered your product or service and have a basic knowledge of what it offers, but haven't engaged further.

- **Interested**: Potential customers show interest by seeking more information about your product or service. They start to perceive how it might meet their needs or solve a problem. If they've contacted you or signed up for information, consider them a "lead."

- **Evaluating**: At this point, potential customers compare your offering with others in the market and consider factors like features, benefits, price, and quality to determine if it's the right choice. Their intellect is getting primed by your technical information.

- **Committed**: You've got them on the hook! They have decided that your product or service is the right choice and are prepared to make a purchase. They may be finalizing decisions on specifics like quantity, service levels, or terms.

- **Action**: This stage involves the actual purchase or signing up for your service. The customer transitions from a prospective buyer to an actual customer.

- **Advocate**: After the purchase, satisfied customers promote your product or service through word-of-mouth, reviews, or testimonials, influencing others in their network.

Aligning these categories to their messaging needs in a similar way to how Maslow's hierarchy can ebb and flow over a growth cycle could look something like the diagram below:

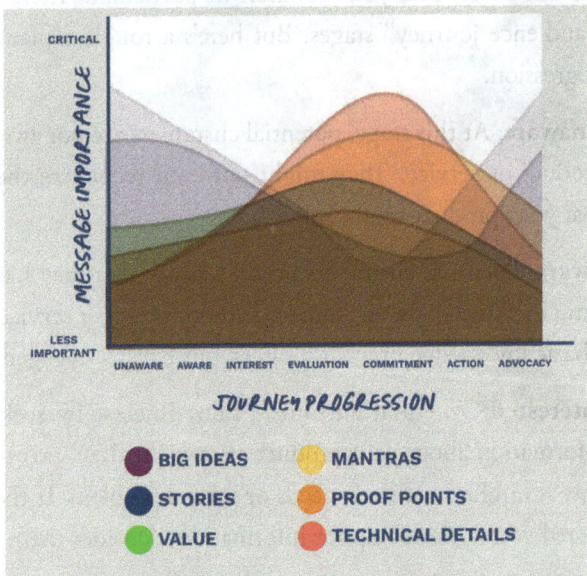

Figure 11: Messaging needs along an audience journey

Let's talk through each messaging element and why they're plotted the way they are.

Unaware Audiences

At this stage, the primary goal is to grab attention and create emotional engagement. Big Ideas should be boland inspirational, providing a compelling reason for the audience to pay attention. You can introduce stories that resonate emotionally, illustrating relatable problems and aspirational outcomes.

A small set of very clear Value propositions is crucial here. They don't need to be all that you've identified. They should be entry-level ones, so to speak, the most common and compelling to all intended audiences.

This is where heavy use of those Mantras—catchy and memorable phrases that reflect the audience's values and aspirations—create emotion and logic.

Aware Audiences

Once an audience is aware, reinforce the initial emotional connection by echoing the Big Ideas in most messaging. This makes sure the audience remembers why they should care. Continue building emotional connections while starting to introduce Story elements that demonstrate credibility. Begin highlighting the tangible and intangible benefits your product or service offers, addressing the audience's initial logical queries.

Interested Audiences

As engagement with the audience develops, deepen the narrative with more detailed stories that showcase your understanding of the audience's challenges and your unique solutions. You can tailor use cases and case studies to their particular experiences.

Provide clear, logical explanations of how your solution addresses the audience's needs and the value that they will receive. This can also be a great time to introduce testimonials, case studies, and third-party validations to build trust.

Evaluating Audiences

The evaluating audience is one whose attention and interest you've captured, but they're comparing you to other options or to existing solutions that they're aware of. They're not always doing a direct "bake-off" between you and other competing directions, but it's likely they're doing so subconsciously. So now is the time to begin providing contrast with your competition. It's worth noting that "doing nothing" is often an option for your audience, and it's typically easier. So remember to position yourself against the status quo in addition to competition.

You can do this by continuing to focus heavily on the logical aspects of your offering, emphasizing unique selling points, benefits, and competitive advantages. And begin providing detailed case studies, performance metrics, and industry certifications to substantiate claims and build credibility. Now is the time to offer comprehensive technical details to satisfy in-depth evaluations and comparisons.

Committed Audiences

While you may have an audience in a state of commitment, you might need them to begin advocating for your technology to others. This is where you'll begin to see an uptick in the importance of Big Ideas. Remind them of the emotional draw and connection—the why—that made them pay attention to you in the first place.

Reiterate key benefits and proof points to reinforce the decision to choose your solution and equip them to go to bat for you with their stakeholders. Provide additional testimonials and success stories to reinforce trust and confidence in their decision.

You may also be under more technical scrutiny at this point, as many people make decisions emotionally first and then try to justify doing so with logic. Ensure all technical questions are answered comprehensively to facilitate the purchase or implementation process.

Buying and Acting Audiences

Buying or acting audiences continue to need the same messages as they did during consideration. But they could also use some Stories to rekindle the excitement about what they'll be able to accomplish.

Advocates

Once a customer is satisfied, you want their people to become advocates. These folks play a pivotal supporting role in making more customers or bringing more allies to your cause. What's fun about advocates is that they are on your team and part of your community now, sharing the Big Ideas, Stories, and Mantras that will get unaware audiences excited. What's more, they become Proof Points themselves!

What's the reason for the decline and rise in the importance of Big Ideas and Stories as someone moves from Commitment to Action and Advocacy?

The actual customer experience is not a linear path from white paper to the sale. There's an old sales adage that says, "People buy with emotion and justify with logic." While that's true, it never hurts to seal the deal with a reminder of the emotional motivations that captured an audience's attention in the first place.

As covered in chapter 4, remember that people are more likely to develop a bias toward decisions that are easy and simple. Emotions lock in decisions!

Before We Move On:

If you haven't taken the time to consider your audience's journey, now would be a good time. Consider:

1. How do people typically "find you?"

2. Where do you have most of your introductory conversations?

3. What knowledge or experiences are people bringing to you?

4. Are you able to get people to repeat key phrases that you introduce?

5. What have your clients or customers told you about their experiences with you?

6. If someone has ever referred you to someone else, how did they phrase it?

Even if you're not directly involved in "sales," nearly every interaction you have with someone should be done with an understanding of what the next step is.

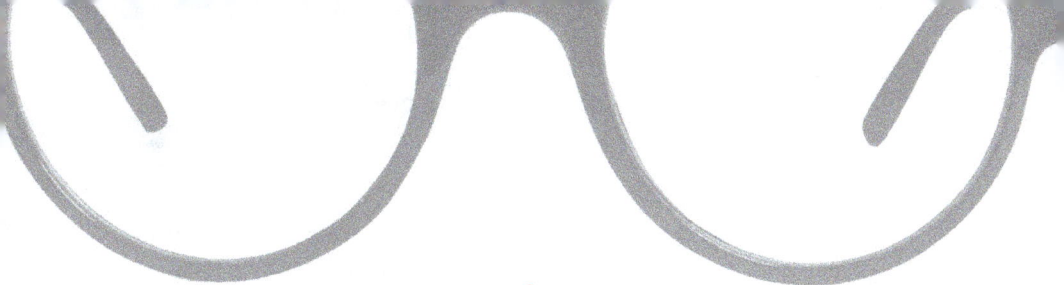

Everything You Could Say (and What You Should)

Documenting the Universe of Possible Messages

*"There are, as you say, bits of eloquence in this book; but
they are drowned in declamations and repetitions.
In the long run, it has the secret of boring people on the
most interesting subject."*

Voltaire
French philosopher, writer, and satirist in a 1770
letter to The Marquis of Villevieille

Let's take a look at each part of a well-balanced breakfast—I mean message
diet. We'll use a combination of the Heart, Head, and Gut Model and
six different types of message elements, each with its own unique set of

qualities.

To illustrate this, I will include a few sample card prompts from the MessageDeck™ marketing card deck, which implements this model in a fun and engaging way (we'll look more deeply at how the MessageDeck can be used as a discovery tool and why the model works so well in a sample workshop in an upcoming chapter).[49] For now, let's just familiarize ourselves with each level of the model and the differences between each category.

Pencils Down!

As we walk through the cards and sample prompts here, you may be tempted to begin frantically scribbling down messaging ideas. If something does come to you, use the pre-assessment worksheet found at nerdthattalksgood.com/goodies to capture anything that's particularly burning.

But what we're doing right now is about learning, not doing. So, it's okay to just step through the model.

Ideas

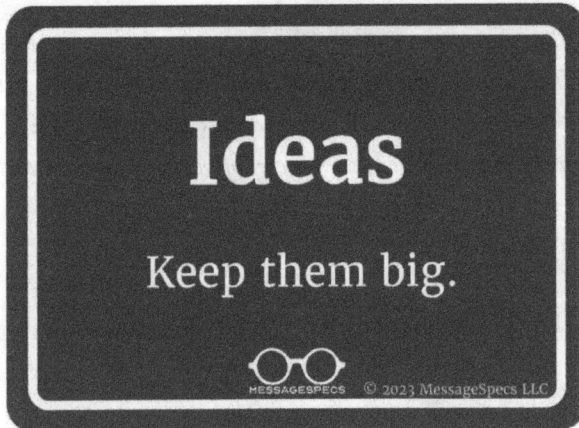

Figure 12. Category 1 - Big Ideas

---

[49] For more information on, and samples of, the deck, go to nerdthattalksgood.com/messagedeck. Use the coupon code at the back of this book for a discount, just for being awesome!

First up, the **Big Ideas**. These are the sweeping, thematic things that should permeate a full brand story or messaging.

This is your "big why" and is the most important thing an audience should take away after a first encounter. After all, if you're not hooking them emotionally right off the top, you may not be able to hold their attention when moving toward "deeper" subjects.

Big Ideas should answer questions like:

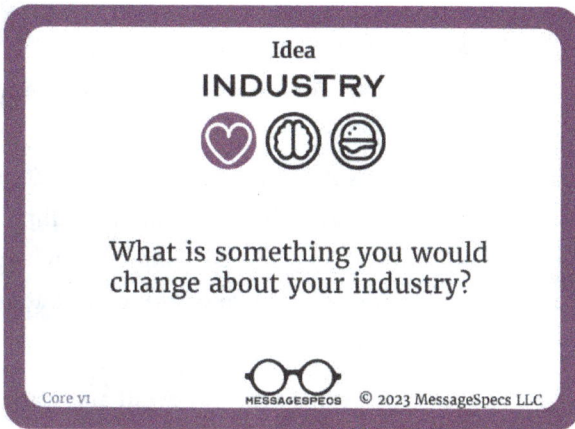

Figure 13. Pushing back on the conventional or status quo

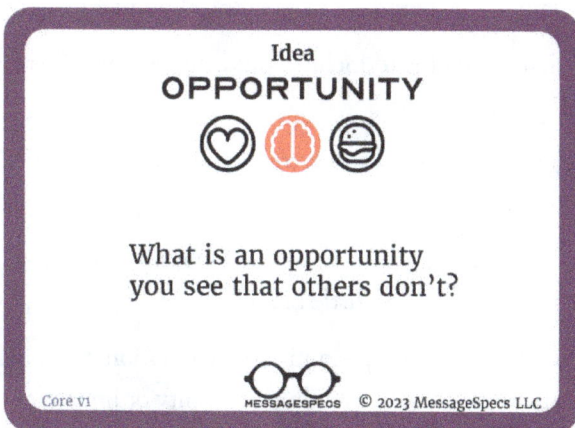

Figure 14. What you're bringing to the market that nobody else is

Idea

ADVOCATE

What or for whom do you advocate?

Core v1   MESSAGESPECS   © 2023 MessageSpecs LLC

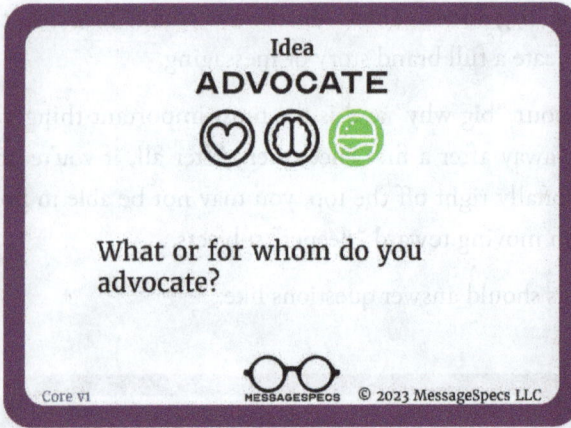

Figure 15. Staking a claim for a particular market segment

Note that each prompt has the heart, head, or gut icon indicated. In general, you want your Big Ideas to be bold and compelling enough to generate emotion in an audience at first encounter, though it's okay for them to focus on a particular objective like sparking inspiration (head) or building immediate trust (gut).

Just avoid falling in love with a technical detail and using it as a Big Idea. A feature or capability is rarely a big enough umbrella idea to carry a full message forward. Sure, there are exceptions, but there are also pitfalls to hooking your whole brand up to a technical point.

If your first instinct is to include anything technical here, take a step back and ask a few questions:

- *Why do I think this technical detail elicits an emotional response?* Dig deeper to see if it can be articulated simply and without jargon.

- *Is this a universal idea that appeals to my target audience, or just me?* This involves doing a little bias checking.

Big Ideas should be unique and largely emotional, though they can have secondary objectives like creating credibility or imparting a big, technical "wow" moment. Ideally, keep your final Big Ideas to two or three that should be tightly related.

The Periodic Table of Bad B2B Big Ideas

Many founders or product teams absolutely fall in love with a Big Idea, going so far as using it as their tagline—without validating whether it's unique in their market.

How many times have you seen these Big Ideas walking through a conference or browsing B2B websites:

- *Revolutionizing _____*
- *We do _____ so you can focus on _____*
- *Our _____, your success*
- *Do more _____ with less _____*
- *Our mission is your mission*

You may even be using one of these in your messaging now—because it sounds good. Saying your Big Idea to yourself, you nod and go, "Yeah, that sounds like us!"

But we've been conditioned to hear these tropes and clichés and mindlessly nod along. It's not that they are particularly wrong. They're just *everywhere*, which is why they sound and feel so good.

There are several "types" of these Big Ideas, and I've included a table in Part Four of this book organized under a super set of "families."

If you gravitate toward one of these commodified Big Ideas, use the table to consider what the root thought behind it is and then come up with an original way to express it.

Stories

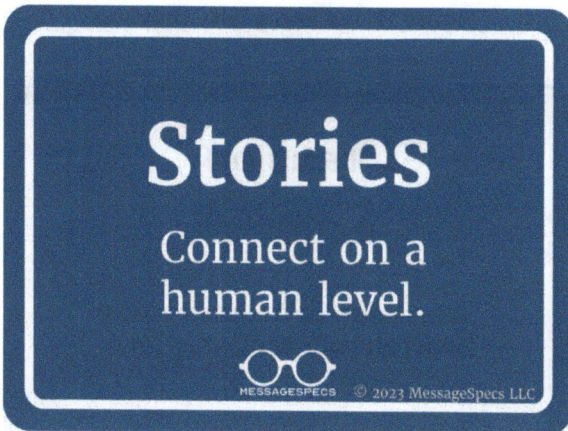

Figure 16. Category 2 – Stories

Marketing "thought leaders" have pontificated ad nauseam about Joseph Campbell and the hero's journey, to the point where "brand storytelling" has become a productized tactic and not a root principle.

Stories are, at their basic level, how we connect with the day-to-day lived experiences of our audience. It's how we demonstrate empathy and share what makes us tick.

A good story connects on an emotional level. A great one does it while building credibility. Stories should dig into things like:

Figure 17. We know who they are

Figure 18. Demonstrate empathy and understanding of relationship dynamics

Figure 19. The "eureka!" moment

Each of these has little to do with what you're ultimately selling or offering, but they have a lot to do with the context in which you're doing it.

Storytelling is all about placing yourself within a narrative moment for the audience. How do you fit into *their* experience? How can you make them see your solution as part of their story? Don't go all metaphorical Obi-Wan Kenobi on them, but do show them how your approach/product/solution delivers the happy ending for them.

From Someone Smarter than Me

In his first book *The Storytelling Animal*, English professor and author Jonathan Gottschall explores how stories make us human. He asks questions like, "Is story-telling a biological imperative?" He also shows interesting research and personal stories about how storytelling brings us together into communities.[50]

He spends some time on what social scientists call "fictional screen media" (television commercials) making my point above better than I do:

- Laundry detergent commercials show overworked parents struggling with mountains of dirty socks.
- Home security companies build up moments of fear with shadowy prowlers.
- Snack companies bring back familiar, sympathetic characters from previous campaigns.

---

[50] Jonathan Gottschall, *The Storytelling Animal: How Stories Make Us Human* (Mariner Books, 2013).

These story types are usually common in direct-to-consumer or commercial packaged goods. Why should B2B marketing and technical communications be any different?

Values

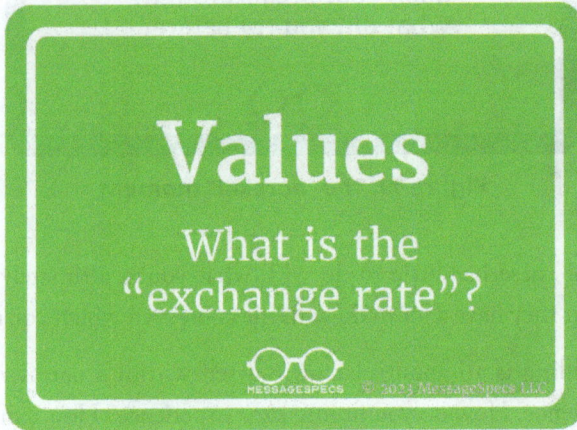

Figure 20. Category 3 – Values

These are not corporate "mission, vision, value" stuff.[51]

The **Values** I'm talking about are "value propositions"—clear articulations of what you're offering. What is the audience going to get out of listening to you? Values often come not from your perspective but are developed by listening closely to your audience. What is it they want (or don't want)?

---

[51] Just to confuse things, typical corporate boilerplate mission, vision, and values fit better in the Story or Mantra categories.

Values answer the classic "what's in it for me?" questions, like:

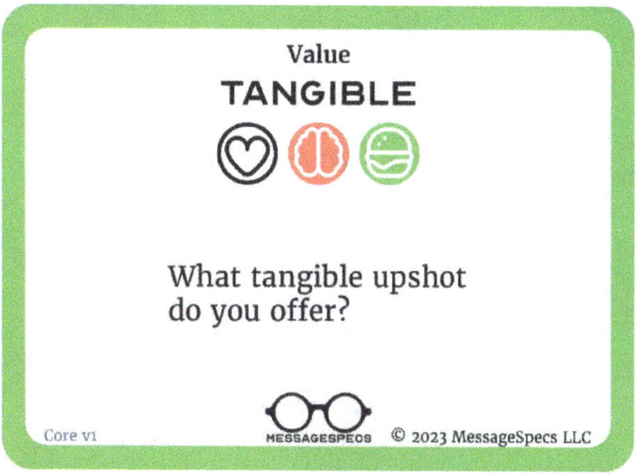

Figure 21. Concrete and measurable benefits

Figure 22. Less measurable but still important benefits

Value
PAY IT FORWARD

What downstream benefits do
your customers' customers
receive because of you?

Core v1   MESSAGESPECS   © 2023 MessageSpecs LLC

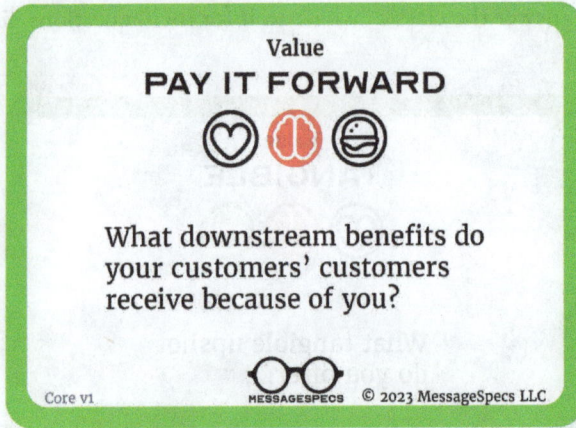

**Figure 23. Indirect value to customers in
the eyes of their stakeholders**

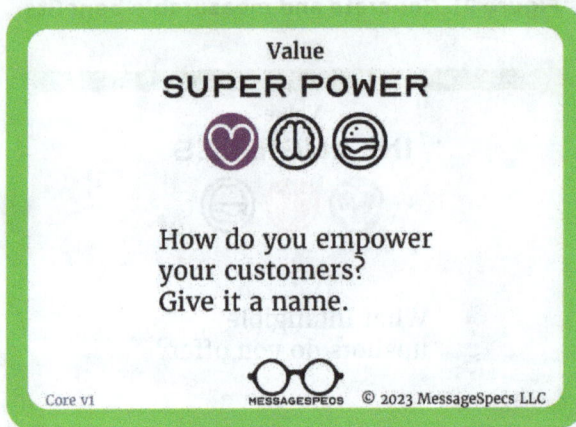

Value
SUPER POWER

How do you empower
your customers?
Give it a name.

Core v1   MESSAGESPECS   © 2023 MessageSpecs LLC

**Figure 24. Superpowers, by the way, pair very nicely
with a villain story element. Pow! Zing! Boom!**

It's key to remember when developing Values to have a wide variety of them. Notice that the above examples run the gamut from tangible to intangible, quantitative to qualitative, and even emotional.

Depending on the audience, you'll need to carefully consider their motivating factors and what they desire. Even the most technical audiences have emotional needs. If competing with other options on purely mathematical or metric bases, the one that ekes out a little emotion will generally be selected.

While it's not always possible to be heavily emotional in a technical pitch based on values, you can soften the sell so it doesn't come across as purely transactional.

Mantras

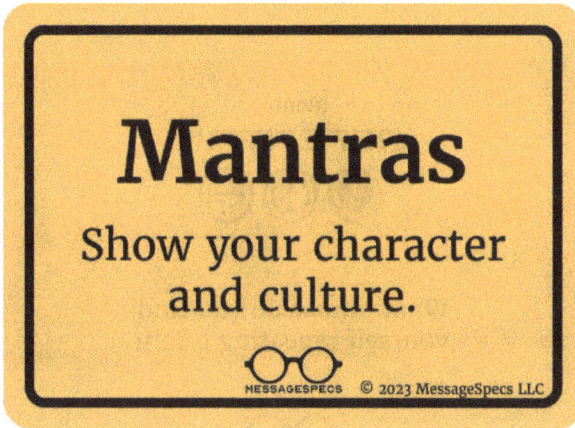

Figure 25. Category 4 – Mantras

The earliest known use of the noun "mantra" was in the late 1700s, borrowing from Sanskrit.

Today, mantras are generally understood to be repeated passages of scripture, philosophy, or other spiritually significant vocalizations used in prayer.

But the concept of mantras has become popular in business as well. The *Cambridge Business English Dictionary* defines a mantra as:

> noun [C]: a word or phrase that is often repeated and that expresses something that people believe in.[52]

For our purposes here, **Mantras** are phrases and concepts burned into

---

[52] *Cambridge Business English Dictionary*, "mantra," accessed January 26, 2025, https://dictionary.cambridge.org/us/dictionary/english/mantra.

a person's character or organizational culture, a way of saying "This is who I am" or "This is who we are."

They can reflect the beliefs of an audience and be used to quickly build credibility and affinity. Almost like saying, "I'm just like you—we have the same frame of reference and speak the same language."

It takes time and homework to discover your mantras and those of a marketplace. But you can find them by observing:

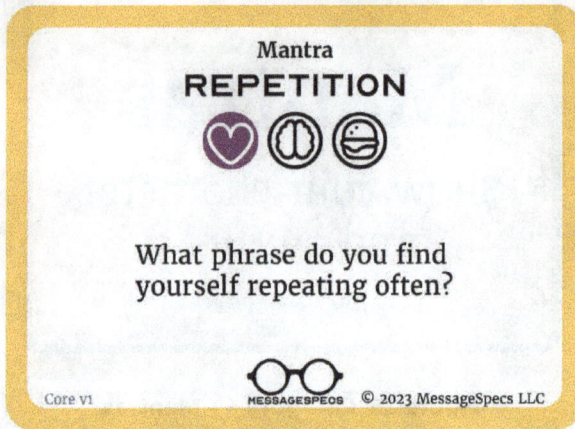

Figure 26. What comes up in daily conversations?

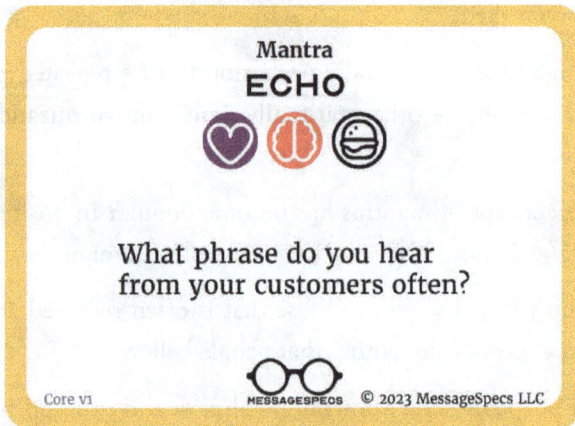

Figure 27. Doing a little snooping on the internet is fine

Figure 28. What's the lingo?

If you have the time and are able, then interacting with customers directly (a lot) is absolutely the best way to discover an audience's internal mantras. If possible, hire a customer validation or research firm. Or use a tool like Gong[53] to capture and sift through customer conversations for patterns.

While they aren't the only source of marketing "taglines" or "slogans," they do make for great ones.

Mantras must be genuine statements of culture and truth about your organization. For example, one of my mantras is "Complex does not have to be confusing." It's a statement of truth, but also represents a deeper "why." It can take a while to find yours, so don't be discouraged if it doesn't happen quickly.

---

[53] While I haven't used it myself, Gong (https://www.gong.io) is a very popular tool in the SaaS field because it passively transcribes customer and prospect interactions, allowing you to pull out trends later.

Proof Points

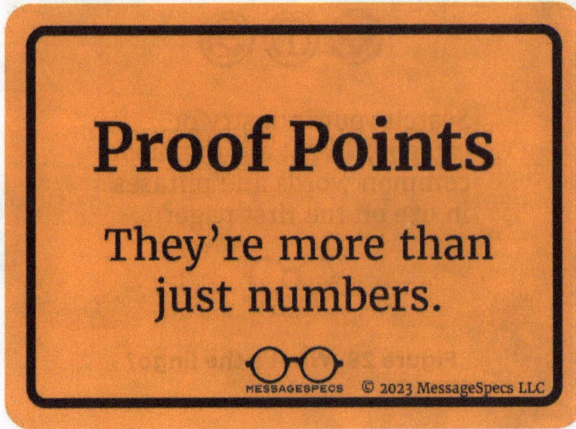

Figure 29. Category 5 - Proof Points

Eventually, an audience's next logical question—"Why should I trust you?"—must be answered.

Where Stories and Mantras did a lot of emotional heavy lifting to build credibility, **Proof Points** go for the gut.

Start capturing (as early as possible) every conceivable proof point in a centralized repository. Things like:

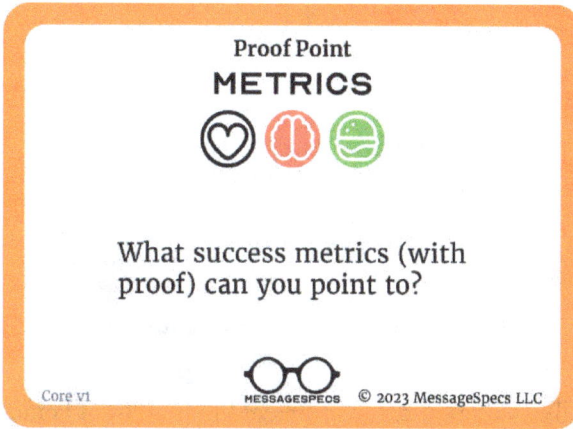

Figure 30. Demonstrate direct and measurable proof

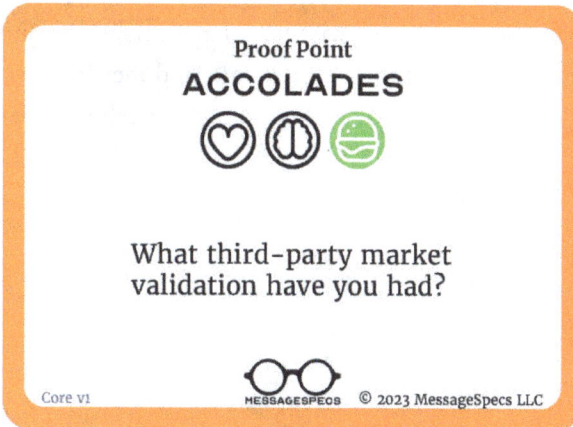

Figure 31. Borrow a little credibility using how others have validated you

Proof Point

TESTIFY!

Talking about yourself is
weird.
What can you get someone
else to say about you?

Core v1 MESSAGESPECS © 2023 MessageSpecs LLC

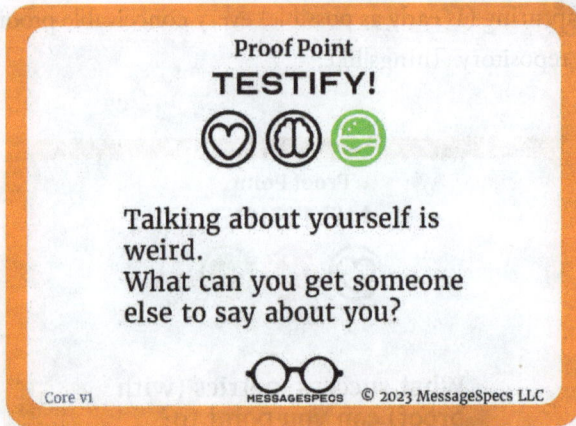

Figure 32. What someone else says about you carries more weight

Again, like Values, there are different kinds of Proof Points to include. Hard ones, like performance metrics and result KPIs, are obvious. Soft social proofs—like testimonials or case-study stories—are also useful.

But when you're making a case for a large perspective shift, look for external proofs like industry reports, trends, and metrics to support your case. These allow you to avoid bragging about yourself while letting someone else's words do it for you.

Technicals

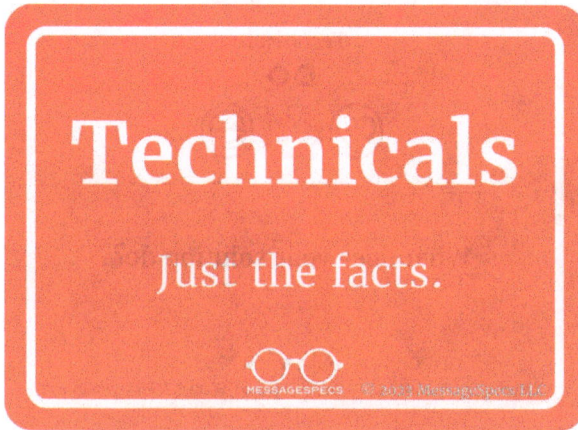

Figure 33. Category 6 – Technicals

Finally, the one you've been waiting for—technical details. Many technologists feel they have these down, but they're often scattered or spread across several pieces of collateral.

Collecting all the details in a catalog of technical messages helps in deciding which ones to use when, and in what balance, against other "lighter" messages.

Yes, you definitely want to answer questions like:

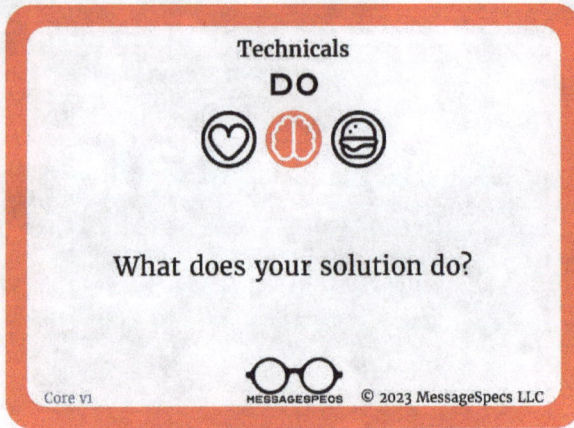

Figure 34. What are you selling?

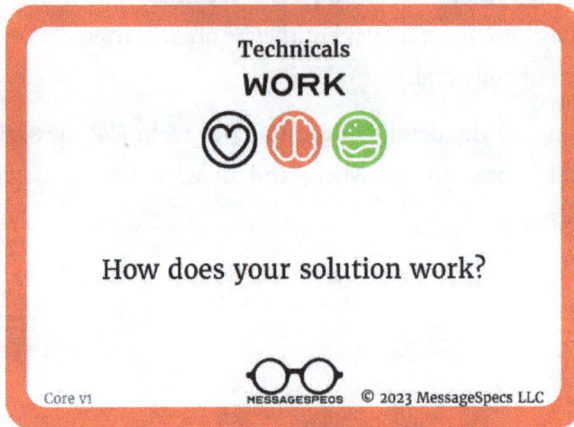

Figure 35. How does it work?

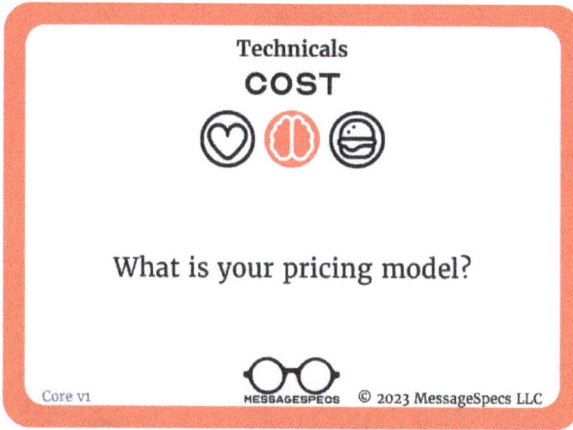

Figure 36. What does it cost/how does someone get it?

Messaging points like these are commodity items, however. They're bare minimum table stakes. You should also be prepared to answer many other questions that are on the audience's mind. So, be ready to answer them with messaging elements. Even with **Technicals**, you need to think outside the box.

Consider documenting other questions like:

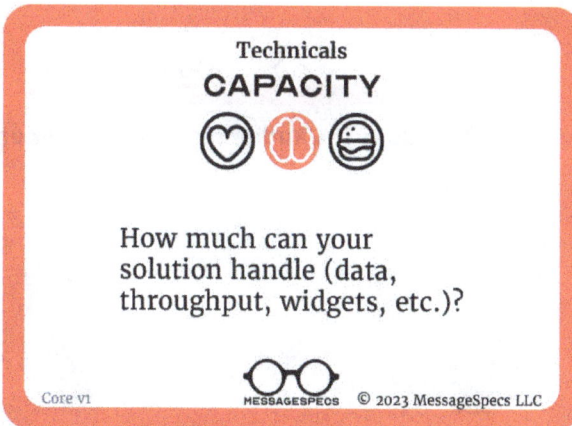

Figure 37. Will it scale?

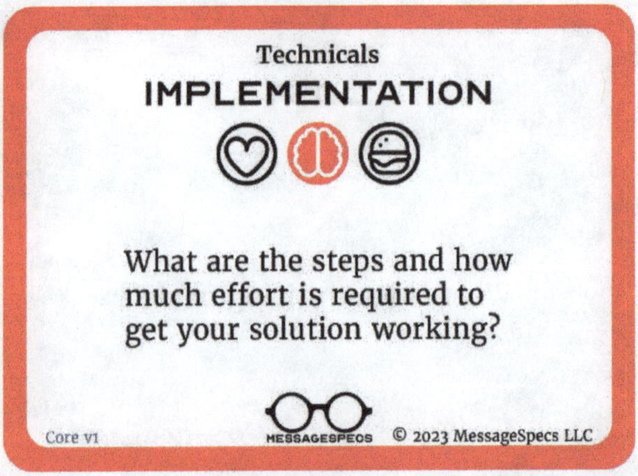

Technicals
IMPLEMENTATION

What are the steps and how much effort is required to get your solution working?

Core v1   MESSAGESPECS   © 2023 MessageSpecs LLC

Figure 38. A story in itself (and can be introduced by one)

Technicals
INTEGRATION

What is required to integrate or use your solution?

Core v1   MESSAGESPECS   © 2023 MessageSpecs LLC

Figure 39. What does the audience need on their end?

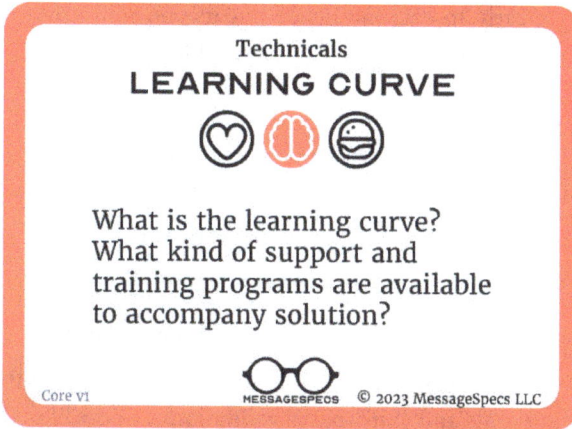

Figure 40. Will the audience need help using what you're selling?

Each of these can be the basis for an entire knowledge base entry or blog article. The important thing is that you've thought through as many as possible and have them documented and at the ready. We'll work on the documentation in Part Three of the book, which covers implementation.

When to Say "When"

How do you know when you have enough (or too many) messages? It depends on your organization, but here are a few good rules of thumb:

- **Big Ideas**: Try to come out of this exercise with no more than three to four Big Ideas. Ideally, one or two should be the most prominent. Merging or adapting messages is always possible if you find they fit better into different (or multiple) categories.

- **Stories**: Depending on the number of discrete target audiences, you may have many different stories, but try to keep to a handful (three to four) per audience. Focus on the core use cases or more prominent experiences of the audience you're seeking to connect with. You can always discover and add more later.

- **Values**: These can get tricky. Make sure two or three values speak very clearly to each audience but use no more than six that are highlighted at "top-level" channels like home pages or introductory content.

- **Mantras**: Pick as many of these as make sense to be authentic to your character/culture and that of the audience. Select a couple to be key to the brand voice. Able to find one that really sings? Consider it as a tagline or slogan.[54]

- **Proof Points**: Quality over quantity here. Make sure you've got enough variety between hard and soft proofs. And collect as many testimonials and third-party validations as possible.

- **Technicals**: Really, this depends on what is on offer. These can be pulled from technical documentation over time, but the key is having the details accessible in one place for team awareness and consistency.

Again, messaging continually evolves. So, if you don't capture every potential messaging point in the beginning, that's okay. That's why we're going to catalog a formal messaging system, which is up next.

---

[54] The difference between a *tagline* and a *slogan* is the difference between *branding* and *marketing*. A tagline generally defines your brand and sticks around much longer, while a slogan can be used more surgically for campaigns or shorter-term needs.

PART THREE

The Battle Plan

Putting It All into Action

The best way to change something is to first take an objective look at what you're already working with. Too many times, I've been asked to help someone come up with "something new" in their messaging before we've unpacked what they're already saying and mined for hidden gems.

We now know the elements of a well-balanced message, and we understand the components of a messaging stack. But before we throw away the old in favor of the new, there might be some gold nuggets hidden in the backlog of half-baked and scattered messaging we had before.

What are some practical ways to assess your current messaging to draw out its more compelling elements before expending energy to come up with something new? That's where we're headed in Part Three. Buckle up and prepare to take a good, hard look in the messaging mirror. Because it's about to get real.

9

Finding Gaps and Opportunities

Knowing What You Know and Don't Know Now, So You Can Know Where to Go Next—You Know?

"The greater the artist, the greater the doubt;
perfect confidence is granted to the less talented as a
consolation prize."

Robert Hughes
Australian art critic and writer

⟨○○⟩

Maybe you have started writing down thoughts based on the Messaging Framework from the previous chapter. Hold onto those notes; we don't need them *quite* yet.

This chapter is about doing the necessary analysis to get a lay of the land. That means understanding how you're messaging today so you can create a catalog of macro-level "stuff"—the raw materials you build on—to help you evaluate moving forward.

When I work with a client, we start with a Content Catalog where I perform an audit of as much material as I can get my hands on. This is to create a 10,000-foot view of the general messaging the client is using across all their communication channels. By chunking up messages and aligning them like for like, duplication, misalignment, and missing items can be seen quickly. Sometimes even great diamonds in the rough—pushed to less prominent web pages or print pieces—can be uncovered, polished up, and used as primary messages.

Consistency Is King

I've already written about the importance of consistency, but here's an example. I recently did a client messaging review across their website and sales collateral. All told, they had:

- One mission statement
- One vision statement
- One purpose statement
- One cultural statement
- Five cultural values
- Four business principles
- One pledge to customers with six points (phew!)

These were spread across web pages, slide presentations, print pieces, and even email samples. I challenged them to explain how, as a company, they could find focus when being pulled in so many directions. And how a customer could ever understand what's really driving the company through all the noise.

This is why brevity and consistency across channels are crucial to perfect buyers finding you.

Even slight variations in messages across multiple sources can create subconscious confusion within an audience. Confuse—and you lose.

Why Not "Start Fresh"?

Too many teams go into marketing or messaging strategy meetings "fresh," trying to come up with "something new" to message on. But if you don't first have a clear accounting of the messaging already being put out into the world, whatever new messaging you come up with invariably ends up conflicting or clashing with existing content.

This is classic "build the plane while we're flying it" thinking. A content catalog will help you avoid that when the process of discovering your new messaging is underway.

Creating a Content Catalog

A Content Catalog doesn't need to be anything fancy, but it does take a little bit of hunting and gathering to get everything in one place. To help along the companies I work with, I provide a Google Drive link and a document template[55] and ask them to dump as much stuff on me as possible.

Once I have the content, I sift through each artifact looking for specific qualities of content to populate the template.

These are the categories I use, though you can use any breakdown that makes sense:

- **Brand and Content Guides** – Anything that provides guidance on your brand language, look, and feel.

- **Personas/Audiences** – Any notes or documentation you have on your target audiences and what you know about them.

- **Value Statements** – Any statements or promises you make about the benefits or positive outcomes you can lay claim to.

---

[55] If you want to grab a copy of the same template I use, you can at nerdthattalksgood. com/goodies.

- **Testimonials** – Stuff others have said about you.

- **Proof Points** – Any metrics or outcomes you can directly identify to prove your case, including statistics (yours and from third parties).

- **Features and Capabilities** – The laundry list of technical features and details about your solution or subject.

- **Case Studies** – Documentation or examples of where you've delivered success to others. (Bonus: these are great places to mine for testimonials and proof points. Keep a separate but cross-referenced list.)

- **Differentiators** – How do you know or why do you think you're different than others?

- **Collateral** – A big reference list of all the documents and things you already have, with pointers to where they are, including each one's big takeaway.

Each category provides a place to drop in the bit of copy, statistics, or other nuggets similar enough to one another to be compared for consistency.

For example, you may find several slightly different pieces of copy that function as a positioning statement:

[COMPANY] is a [CATEGORY] for [CONSUMER] that [DOES A THING].

If so, copy them all into the Brand and Content Guides section.

See several statements of customer benefit or outcomes? Dump them into the Value Statements category. And so on.

You might notice some of them also fit into levels of the message pyramid. Go ahead and tag them or make a note. It's not crucial to tag or force them into alignment with any particular objective or level just yet; the exercise here is just to get everything in one place.

If you haven't already, head over to this book's Goodies page and download the sample Content Catalog worksheet now at nerdthattalksgood.com/goodies.

Now, Take a Step Back

Once you've copied over every bit of content that can be categorized, it's a good idea to give your brain a little space and let it cool down. This will help you to be objective when it comes to doing an assessment.

After some time away from the catalog, try to look at each section to see whether you're able to discern slight differences in overlapping messages or even identify old or contradictory material. If something doesn't jibe[56] with the rest of the content, remove it.

You may begin to see some rough outlines of things that could become Big Ideas or Story elements. Likely, there'll be some sections without any entries at all, like Proof Points and Value Statements.

Now you know where to put your energy as we start discovering how to fill the gaps and seize messaging opportunities!

---

[56] Public service announcement: The correct phrase is "jibe with," not "jive with." Jibe likely comes from an old sailing term that means to move back and forth, adjusting to changing water and wind conditions. As a verb, jive means to dance. Thank you for coming to my TED Talk.

10

Have Fun with Your Messaging

From Ants to Analysis and Everything in Between

"Please do not take life quite so seriously—you surely will never get out of it alive."

Elbert Hubbard
American writer, publisher, and humorist

◠◡

When I made the jump from government communications to marketing, I saw a major shift in my involvement with clients as a "creative." As an in-house communicator, I worked day in and day out directly with practitioners, developers, and other technical leaders. As soon as I put on a marketing hat, I was almost exclusively put in front of sales, marketers, and corporate leadership to help them communicate technical messaging.

It was almost like people didn't trust the nerds to have the goods.

But on the rare occasion that I worked directly with a founder or lead developer—and given time to truly dig into the technology—we discovered hidden messages and stories overlooked in many "brand discovery" sessions.

For example, a sales or marketing person could tell me how a prospect might use their tool to address a pain point. But the developer who built the tool could tell me why they implemented the solution in a particular way and what they'd tried before. This insight helped me craft use case narratives that showed prospects that we truly had been in their shoes before and were not just parroting back talking points.

So, it wasn't that the techies didn't have great input—though they usually weren't given the chance to contribute. It also wasn't the case that technical interactions alone produced the input for creating fully-formed messaging, which is why some technical founders couldn't seem to take on the dual role of builder and seller.

What I realized was that developing truly unique messaging requires full-spectrum team input to populate the full spectrum of messaging needs. I also knew it would take a lot of time to have all the conversations I needed to gather all the input I needed to create fully-formed messaging.

As a brand and content strategist, I began collecting a list of prompts and thought experiments to sneak into conversations and opportunistic interactions with clients. These helped elicit the gold-nugget input I needed to create unified big brand ideas backed up by deep technical marketing content.

The list slowly grew into the hundreds. I kept it in a spreadsheet I could quickly reference. Over time, it coalesced into the Message Pyramid layers covered in chapter 5. Eventually, that list turned into a set of tabletop cards that teams could use to gamify their messaging.

But Why a Game?

Before introducing the MessageDeck and method, I'd like to share a bit more about my startup and the first card deck I created.

As I alluded to in the Introduction, I had a brief career layover as the product evangelist and director of marketing and communications for an early-stage cybersecurity company. The product was a new class of risk quantification platforms. Gartner, the analyst firm that plays kingmaker in the industry by defining entire categories and declaring companies as "Cool Vendors," had only just begun to talk about the topic a year or so prior.[57]

We were solving a newly defined problem in a crowded marketplace, using a novel technological approach birthed out of academia.

To complicate matters, the product's "secret sauce" was based on the founder's PhD thesis. Simply put (ha!), it was a highly complex artificial intelligence algorithm based on the behavior of ant swarms.

Our challenge was to quickly explain everything from *who, why, how*, and *what* to audiences still used to fifteen-year-old techniques. It wasn't easy.

At the time, this was our best "brief explainer":

> Emergent's Instinct Engine™ allows companies to see around the corner and identify the digital risks most likely to impact them tomorrow. Using advanced machine learning and emergent AI risk algorithms, it explores hundreds of thousands of loss scenarios to identify the cyber intrusions that could create the biggest impacts.
>
> We use a biologically-inspired swarming approach to identify the most likely attack paths to your greatest risks—and those that cause the most damage—so you can reduce your risk before an incident happens. Our solution enables business owners to understand the amount of cyber risk to which they are exposed and

---

[57] By the way, my company was selected as a Cool Vendor in the first group of companies in the space <toots own horn> … right before we ran out of runway <sad trombone>.

for which they are responsible in a dollar-based impact amount.

Not bad. But not exactly a quick and easy elevator pitch.[58] Plus, look at all these complex messaging elements:

- "advanced machine learning and emergent risk algorithms"

- "biologically-inspired swarming approach"

- "reduce your risk before an incident happens"

Cliché after buzzwords after cliché! Ugh! Some were really great ideas on their own. But they were thrown together into a *cluster thought*[59] that we hoped and prayed the audience could parse meaning from.

One day, my eight-year-old son Liam asked me, "Dad, what does your company even do?" So far, I had been unable to explain a PhD-level concept to some of the smartest and highest-paid executives at some of the biggest banks in the country. And now I had to explain it to an eight year old?

As the head of marketing, I was always asked to "show the algorithm." I would turn to the developers for help and be shown math.[60]

Now, Liam is incredibly smart at math, but he wasn't ready for college-level math. He does have a lifelong love of games, however. He's been playing chess since he was three (and beating me since he was five).

So, I grabbed some blank playing cards, a marker, and a handful of plastic ants[61] and, on our kitchen table, laid out what the algorithm "looked" like in my head.

---

[58] I am actually on the record as being vehemently against "elevator pitches," as demonstrated by several social media posts, interviews, and workshop rants, like this one: nerdthattalksgood.com/elevator-pitch.

[59] A "cluster thought" is when you try to jam too many discrete thoughts into a single sentence or paragraph. Copyright, trademark, patents, and all the good things pending.

[60] Not the easiest thing for a former theater school dropout to visualize.

[61] Because, of course, I had those lying around for marketing reasons.

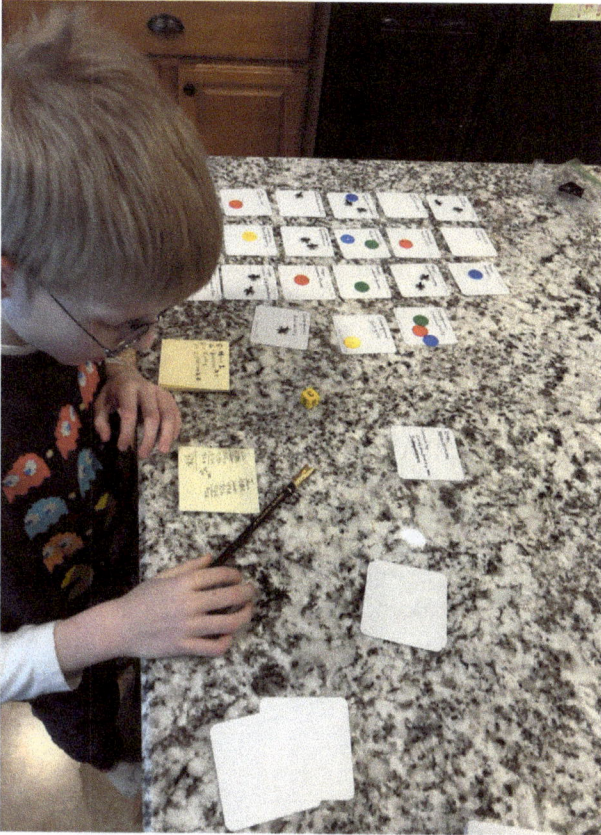

Figure 41. Liam helping me "game out" the ant algorithm

That night, we gamed out several cybersecurity risk scenarios and used the ants to "discover" the most probable and costly ones.

Thinking I was onto something, I mocked up some card designs a month later and printed two prototype decks just before the RSA[62] Conference in San Francisco, California.

Our lead developer saw the cards and said, "Well, actually, that's not how the graphing algorithm works. It's more like …." (I sort of tuned him

---

[62] RSA is one of the largest and most prominent cybersecurity industry conferences, drawing upward of 40,000 attendees and commanding a fee of hundreds of thousands of dollars for an exhibit booth.

out at this point.)[63]

The sales team saw the cards and was skeptical. "You *seriously* want to play cards with the chief risk officer of [insert name of BigHugeNational Bank here]??"

"Yes," I responded.

The point was not to *teach*. The point was to *engage*. I had realized people needed to be leaning in—*wanting* to learn more—before they could learn.

With a copy of the cards in our hands, the company's founder and I walked out onto the RSA floor to attend our scheduled meetings with prospects and potential investors.

---

[63] Only kidding. I love you, man!

Figure 42. CEO Earl with the very first prototype of the Emergynt Risk Deck

Whenever I walked up to a vendor's booth, I listened to their pitch[64] and nodded (I was in field research mode, after all).

When they finally got around to asking me what my company did, I would pull out the cards and tell them a story about how security practitioners often looked at security one way but how executive board members and C-suite leaders needed a different set of answers.

I'd show them a familiar hack scenario as a frame of reference using

---

[64] For some reason, many booth staffers always seem to want to launch into their sales pitch first, before they know anything about who they're pitching to.

the cards. Then had them randomly draw cards to see if the deck could create a hack they hadn't seen before or one that they felt was impossible.

Each time, their eyes lit up as—hack after hack—this little deck of cards created real-world scenarios. Some of these were on the front page of the newspaper. Some had never been experienced before (or at least disclosed). But an experienced cyber professional could imagine how even the most random scenario was plausible, and even probable! Right there, I was demonstrating the generative[65] and the predictive aspects of the model without ever having to use a buzzword.

Then, with them in the palm of my hand, I would introduce the "cherry on top" cards (also in the palm of my hand). The model contained a set of cards that could be used to estimate the business impact—information that business leaders like a CEO, risk officer, or board members really needed to know.

All this in about 45 seconds. And without ever saying *"multi-nodal artificial intelligence modeled after the behavior of eusocial insects."*

Looking around, I realized that other booth staff and convention attendees were gathering around as I did the little card demonstration. I had effectively done a booth takeover from massive companies like Google, Amazon, and Microsoft.

We were onto something.

Earl reported back that his meetings had gone similarly.

At the next RSA Conference, we submitted a workshop proposal to teach cybersecurity risk modeling using the cards—which resulted in a "sold out" room with dozens of professionals (and potential customers)—where we walked through several activities using the cards as a learning and communication tool.

---

[65] We were doing "generative artificial intelligence" before there was a popular phrase for it. Our developers called it "machine imagination," which sounds very quaint today.

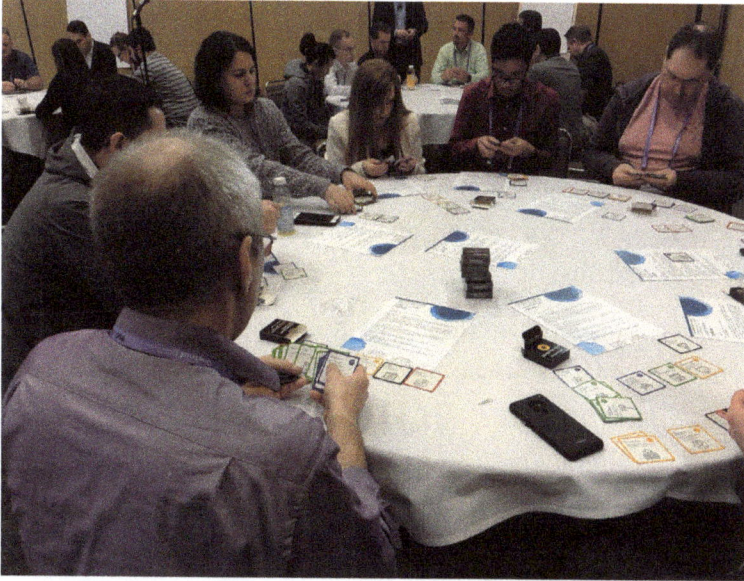

Figure 43. The RSA "Let's Make Risk a Game!" workshop

We followed that up with workshops for the International Information System Security Certification Consortium[66] and Carnegie Mellon University's Heinz College of Information Systems and Public Policy.[67]

We knew we had something interesting on our hands. What we didn't anticipate was how differently everyone would use the cards in the workshops.

Because everyone learns and engages differently, we'd created a way to showcase the power of the solution that let the product get out of the way so people could discover and experience it for themselves.

---

[66] ISC2 (isc2.org) is a nonprofit organization that specializes in training and certifications for cybersecurity professionals. They issue industry-leading certificates, like the Certified Information Systems Security Professional (CISSP), which is the security equivalent of a Certified Public Accountant (CPA). So, a pretty big honor to present there!

[67] Students in CMU's CISO program still use a version of the cards today.

Thinking with Our Hands

Since then, I've become fascinated with all aspects of workshop facilitation and using card decks as a way of communicating with individuals and groups. I stumbled on a monthly teleconference of card aficionados called Cardstock, where card creators and workshop designers meet to discuss their latest finds and discoveries.

It was at one of these that I met Rina Atienza, a cultural ecologist, community builder, and educator at Kingston University in London.

I interviewed her for this book and for *Nerds That Talk Good* and asked her why cards seemed to unlock things in our thinking that other facilitation methods—surveys, interviews, etc.—don't. She said that they make us aware that ideas are just extensions of ourselves:

> We can let go of them easily or shuffle them and change them and so not be beholden to them. When you have Zoom conversations or meetings, there'll be a flat screen and then you'll read stuff. All the interactions live in your head.
>
> When you physicalize [thoughts] into artifacts, into handheld things—Post-its, or notes—there's a sense of the physical reality and it makes us aware of their temporality, but also just the fact that, we don't have to be stuck to them.[68]

By offloading some of the thinking and message manipulation to the tabletop, we can lessen our mental load and explore more freely.

Looking back, I now know that what I stumbled onto was something called kinesthetic learning.

---

[68] Rina Atienza, personal conversation with the author. Check out the published podcast here: https://nerdthattalksgood.com/podcast/nttg_016/.

Also known as "tactile learning," it is a way in which individuals learn more effectively through physical activities and hands-on experiences. Unlike auditory or visual learners—who learn best through listening to lectures or viewing images and demonstrations—kinesthetic learners thrive when they can move, touch, and do. This is also why you'll see many people moving their hands in a pantomime while explaining a physical concept.

Kinesthetic learners absorb information by being actively involved in the learning process. This often involves activities like building models, experimenting, or engaging in role-playing exercises. Movement can be a crucial part of the learning process. People often remember information better when it is associated with an action or physical activity.

It also acts as a "shortcut" in a world where our attention spans are diminishing, by providing breaks and opportunities to move around. Putting something in someone's hands and letting them "get into it" can engage all kinds of learners.

With that in mind, let's look at how we can gamify our message discovery and come up with something really unique that will capture the hearts, heads, and guts of our audience.

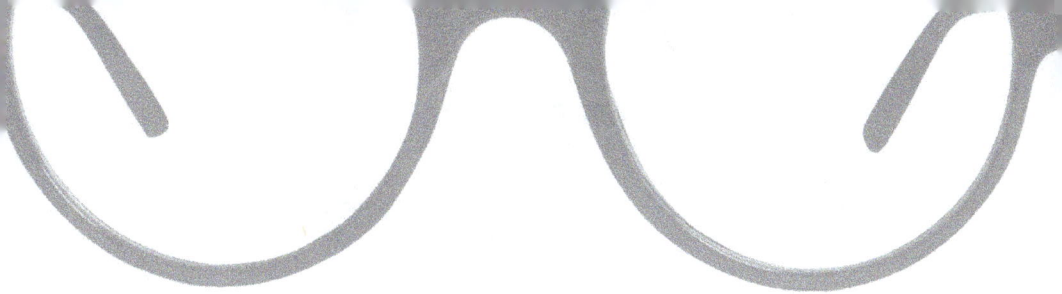

Gamification and Team Alignment

The MessageSpecs Workshop Process

"Shall ... we ... play ... a ... game?"

WOPR
Fictional hyperintelligent war machine
from the movie WarGames

Let's explore ways to deepen technical messaging while considering low-density/high-emotion aspects of well-balanced technical communications—which will help you get noticed, get remembered, and get results.

At the end of this process, you'll have the raw material to create a messaging foundation that can be used to create technical messaging that sticks with an audience and scales beyond just marketing and sales.

This model works both for teams and individuals (I'll call out separately anything that's unique about either approach):

- **Teams**: This activity can be an effective way to engage technical practitioners or cross-functional groups in discovering nontechnical marketing messages. It can be especially appealing to nerds accustomed to technical and structured thinking but who need a way to "hack" their brains into letting go of logic for a while.

When carried out as a team, the activity not only serves as a tool for brainstorming marketing messages but also as a team-building and alignment exercise that can enhance collaboration and understanding across different functions of an organization.

- **Soloists**: This activity can be a great way to clarify personal brands or become a stronger technical presenter because it helps in taking an objective step back to evaluate messaging.

Use the process as a "coach" to push you along a DIY path to create a personal brand's foundation or develop a technical communication style.

Lastly, I'll be using the MessageDeck cards as an example moving forward, though you can do this with or without the cards. There is a list of prompts available on the Goodies link on my web page.[69] There, you can also download the full workshop guide or order your own copy of the cards (digital or physical).

Let's Play!

The MessageSpecs workshop uses card prompts to "trick" participants into lowering their guard and sharing thoughts and feelings—getting things out of their heads and onto the table—so ideas can be shared, discussed, refined, and turned into consistent market messaging.

Here's what a basic MessageDeck card looks like. You'll notice several familiar elements from the Message Pyramid.

---

[69]   Lots of fun things to find at nerdthattalksgood.com/goodies.

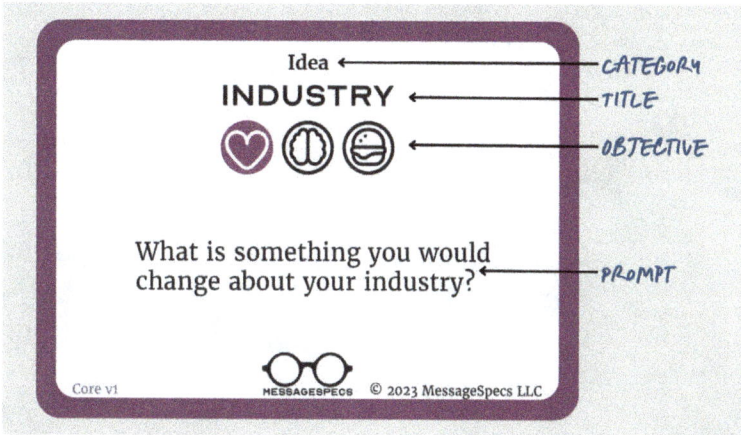

Figure 44. Sample MessageDeck card (this one is a Big Idea)

Each prompt card has a **Category**, **Title**, and **Prompt** that tells you where the card belongs in the exercises covered below and what to do with it.

Some cards have **Objectives**, which provide some guidance on which kind of reaction you should try to create with an audience—the **heart**, **head**, or **gut**. The emoji that's filled in indicates the objective you should target the most with answers.

Select, Collect, Cluster, Cull

The process of discovering your strongest, most authentic messages—the ones that often get overlooked when flipping your head into "marketing mode"—follows four basic steps.[70]

---

[70] Like a good nerd, I could be tempted to call this the SC³ Method, but I'll spare you another acronym to learn.

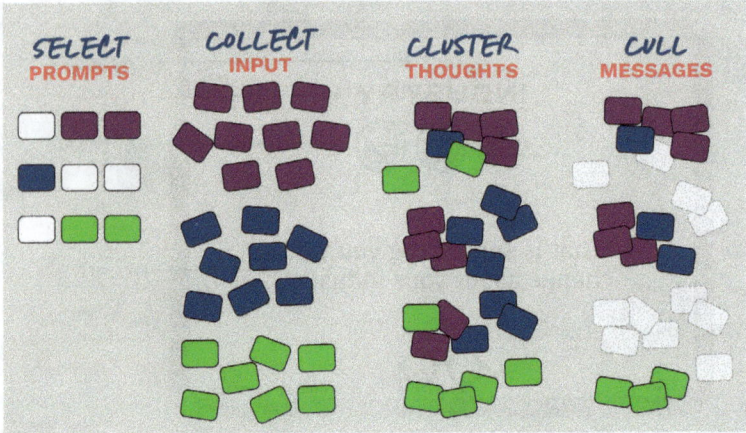

Figure 45. Trust the process

1. Selecting Prompts

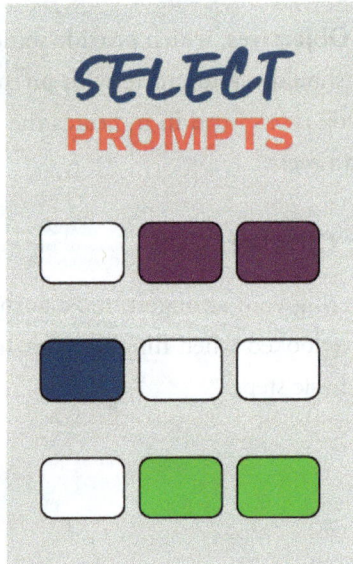

Figure 46. Select a subset of prompts to answer

A workshop's opening involves pulling cards from the MessageDeck or picking prompts from the worksheet. This can be done from top to bottom or randomly using coin flips, dice,[71] mud wrestling, or other feats of strength—whatever works for you.

Categories can be worked one at a time, starting with the Big Ideas and down the messaging pyramid, or things can be done completely randomly. This can be helpful if you have a highly technical group that finds it difficult to jump right in with the "fluffy marketing stuff."

2. Collecting Artifacts

Figure 47. Answer as many prompts as possible in a limited amount of time

As each prompt is revealed, every participant writes down their responses

---

71 A six-sided, multi-colored die can make things very interesting. You can select the stack either by color or number. I found some dice that work just perfectly for the workshop and have made them available at nerdthattalksgood.com/shop.

to be shared with the group. I would not recommend using personal notes or sheets of paper, because it will make following the exercises harder. Use index cards, sticky notes, a digital whiteboard,[72] or anything else that lets you "chunk up" the input later. I personally like color-coded index cards because they're a great way to capture input that can be moved around the table and manipulated by everyone.[73] But be mindful of things like color accessibility.

Figure 48. Small group workshop on the collection step

For example, you may select the Big Gain Idea card.

---

[72] For distributed teams, I have created virtual card canvases that can be experienced remotely. Many groups have used them with great success.
[73] Kinesthetic learning for the win!

Figure 49. The Big Gain card

Take 30 seconds to write down as many positive outcomes or benefits that your solution or subject offers to your audience as you can. Keep thoughts on separate notes or pieces of paper. That is, if you find yourself writing bullet points, break them up!

Next, you pull the Big Pain card.

Figure 50. The Big Pain card

Pains and gains, while related, should elicit slightly different responses. They *can* be mirror images of each other. So try to generate a wholly separate group of responses.

Maybe you pull the Alternative card next.

This takes a little more intellect and logic to respond to than just listing off pains and gains. Come up with as many compelling reasons you can think of (keep them big) that make you stand apart from others in your field.

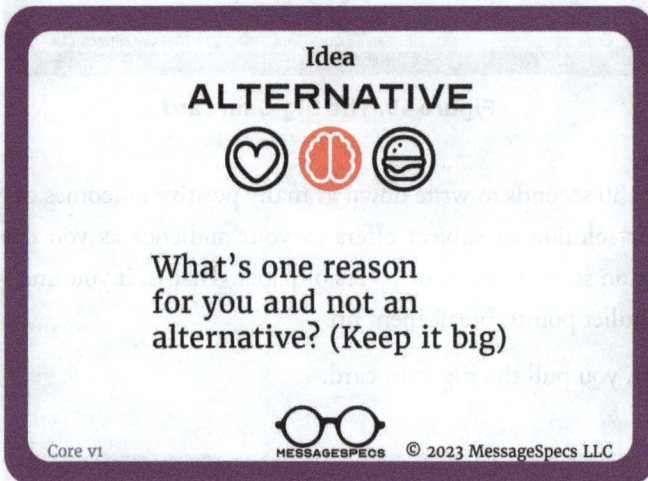

Figure 51. The Alternative card

Lastly, perhaps you pull the Advocate card.

Figure 52. The Advocate card

This is an opportunity for you to think about your audience and how you're especially suited to work with them. For example, you may be an IT managed services provider (MSP). But your primary focus in regard to customers—the ones you really feel called to work with—is independent home builders. Think about why that customer segment is one that you really gel with. Rather than just being "Another MSP," you could be "The Homebuilder's IT Team."

You get the picture. Each card gets your focus for 30 or 40 seconds and you try to generate as many ideas as you can on separate cards, stickies, or rows in a spreadsheet.

Teams Rule #1: No Talking!

Someone on your team may be tempted to start a mini conversation to debate what each prompt means. **It's a trap!**[74]

If this happens, play therapist and answer, "It means whatever you think it means." The goal is to process as many prompts as possible in a short amount of time, letting each participant get whatever is in their head out onto the table in the moment, to be debated and decided on later. Don't get sucked into a back-and-forth discussion.

Many "discovery" workshops or marketing discussions devolve into negotiation sessions where a few voices dominate the time, and important questions get left unasked when time runs out. The objective is to get through as many prompts as possible.

Establish the expectation that nobody is supposed to talk during the first part of the session. With everyone working in parallel, you will generate more artifacts of higher quality in a shorter amount of time.[75]

You don't always have to get through all the prompts, so don't worry about that. After selecting a few prompts at random from each category, you may want to look through the remaining category prompts to select a few specific ones and guide the exercise.[76]

Soloists, Take It Slow!

The advantage of doing this on your own is being able to go at your own pace. The messaging self-discovery can take as long as it needs.

For example, I know of one person who purchased the MessageDeck and spent three months flipping through the cards, answering a single card each day until she had populated an entire virtual whiteboard canvas.

I recommend revisiting the same prompt a few times, several days apart, to see whether you come up with a consistent response. We're different from day to day, so this is a chance to see what's really fundamental to your messaging and what's just a fleeting thought in the moment.

---

[74] Admiral Ackbar, Supreme Commander of the Alliance Fleet, Battle for Endor, year 4 ABY

[75] This is called a "forward-facing activity," where participants don't really interact but are still working together for a common outcome. You can see this in action if you watch two teenagers sit next to one another for hours, playing a video game but never speaking to one another.

[76] This is where the Content Catalog exercise from chapter 8 comes in handy in guiding you toward the cards needed to cover your gaps and opportunities.

Figure 53. A soloist exploring the MessageDeck

3. Clustering Thoughts

Figure 54. Create groups of similar thoughts

Once many artifacts have been created and collected, participants move to the cluster phase—looking through the artifacts collectively for alignment and the creation of groups.[77]

What you're looking for here are similarities in theme, language, or thoughts conveying the same clarity of thought.[78]

It's best to first do this within a common message category to see if you can combine several artifacts into bigger thoughts.

Teams, Let the Conversations Begin!

At this point in group workshops, it's time to begin having conversations. It may be helpful to pair up and work in pairs or gang up one category at a time.

Verbalize why a particular cluster makes sense and what you think the unifying message is.

---

[77] This is also a great time to give your caveman brains a break. Remember Maslow and those physical needs? Have a snack, some water, and walk around a bit. The cards will be there when you're done.

[78] See chapter 2 for an overview of Clarity vs. Focus.

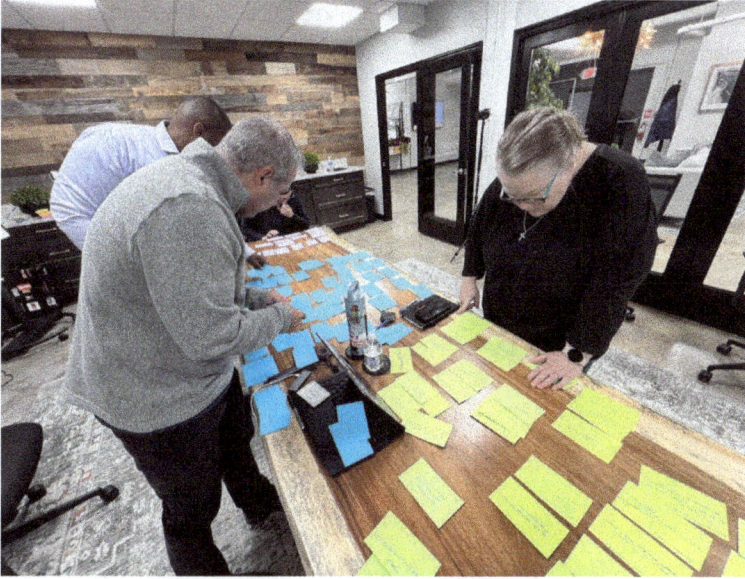

Figure 55. A team on their feet during the clustering exercise

At this point, you can also begin pulling together messages from different categories to create "story stacks" of inputs that loosely fit together and convey larger ideas. In this way, you're testing the inputs to determine whether they feel right when used together. There are some deeper "playbook" activities about building messaging campaigns for specific audiences in Part Four.

Figure 56. Examples of category clustering

The card groups in the figure above are from a virtual workshop I did with the Mozilla Foundation, where we gathered experts from all over the world to explore whether a unified messaging could be created to deal with the growing misinformation challenge.

It may be difficult to see from the above, but even though participants came at the topic from different perspectives, the artifacts were grouped into several clusters.[79] While the words may have been different, the ideas behind the words had a particular theme. The more you can downselect clusters, the better.

---

[79] To see the workshop overview and artifacts in full size, visit nerdthattalksgood.com/musings/cards-against-misinformation.

4. Culling Messages

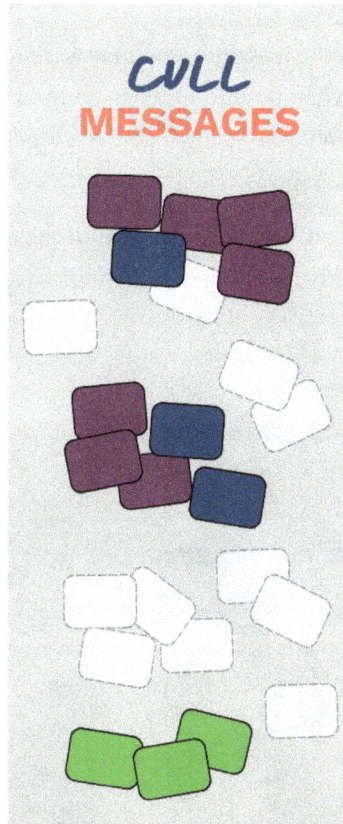

Figure 57. Make decisions about what's in and what's out

Now is the time to begin making some decisions. Be critical of outliers and thoughts that don't seem to fit in with the overall theme of the whole messaging structure. It's okay to discard thoughts at this point. There may also be half-baked thoughts that need to be rewritten or combined.

It's also important to evaluate any messages or themes that are in conflict. Oftentimes, discord between co-founders can become apparent during this exercise. Competing Big Ideas, for example, can result in a fractured message in the marketplace. It's better to hash that out in a workshop than on the clock during an expensive engagement with a branding agency or when serious opportunities are on the line.

Combine (Bonus Round!)

With a downselected set of messages, you may want to try gaming them out with some examples. We'll go into message combos in a later chapter, but you could try a few exercises to string together a Big Idea, a Story, and a few Values to see if you can express a bigger set of thoughts that work together.

When done, you can even arrange them in the top-down hierarchy to see whether they roughly resemble our Message Pyramid.

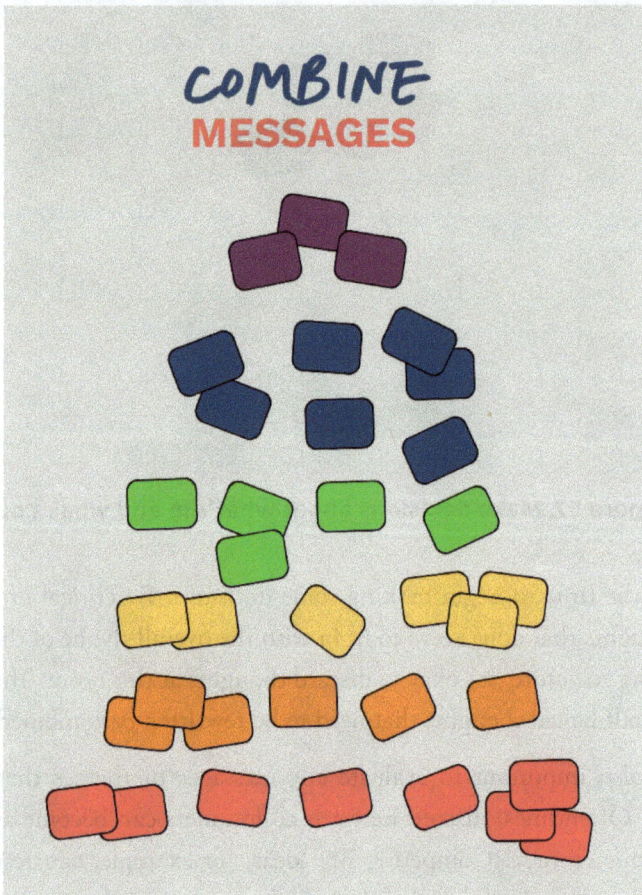

Figure 58. Hey! This looks familiar.

12

Playing Consultant

Check Your Ideas as You Create Them

"Your vision will become clear only when you can look into your own heart. Who looks outside, dreams; who looks inside, awakes."

Carl Jung
Swiss psychiatrist and founder of Analytic Psychology

One of the more difficult things to do as humans is to play self-judge when we're in the moment of creation. Obviously, there are conditions—from the typical "impostor syndrome" to certain clinical diagnoses of paranoia and other maladies—that stop us. What I'm referring to, however, is the ability to step outside oneself and quality control ideas as we're formulating them.

This is one of the advantages of having a facilitated message discovery session. I, as an "interested outsider," can provide instant feedback to the ideas you're putting out onto the table. This could be as simple as asking "why is that?" or "should it be this way?" or even just nodding or shaking my head to silently nudge you into performing a loopback in your mind.

When you're doing the MessageDeck workshop by yourself or trying to lead it as part of a team (with all the baggage that comes with being an insider), it can help to have an outside perspective to allow you to toss in a monkey wrench and disrupt any status-quo thinking.

But how can we introduce the benefit of a dispassionate outsider if we're all insiders?

The Reverse Cards

As I've said before, I'm a bit of a card nerd. After designing the Emergynt Risk Deck, I began collecting card and dice games, trying to unlock techniques and gameplay elements that could be used as forcing mechanisms in my workshops.

One of my favorite games is Mattel's Uno, the classic card game that's brought smiles, laughter, and near fistfights to countless game nights. Uno was dreamed up in 1971 by Merle Robbins, a barber from Reading, Ohio. Inspired by games like Crazy Eights, Merle wanted to create something simple, colorful, and fun for everyone to enjoy.[80]

One of the most exciting cards in Uno is the "Reverse" card—it flips the direction of play, shaking things up and keeping everyone on their toes. Used strategically, Reverse can be one of the more powerful cards in the deck.

So, included in every MessageDeck is a set of special "Focus" cards that I like to refer to as my "Message Reverse" cards. These cards contain prompts that you may deal on top of participant input cards when you need to shake things up a little bit.

Prompts like:

---

[80] "Uno," *The Strong: National Museum of Play*, accessed January 26, 2025, https://www. museumofplay.org/toys/uno/.

Focus

BREAK IT UP!

Break this message down
into separate thoughts.

Core v1   MESSAGESPECS   © 2023 MessageSpecs LLC

**Figure 59. When a notecard has too many thoughts
on it, break them up onto separate cards**

Focus

DISPROVE IT!

Is this universally true?

Play devil's advocate
and see whether you
can disprove it.

Core v1   MESSAGESPECS   © 2023 MessageSpecs LLC

**Figure 60. Check yourself and see whether you can come
up with a counterargument that disproves this thought**

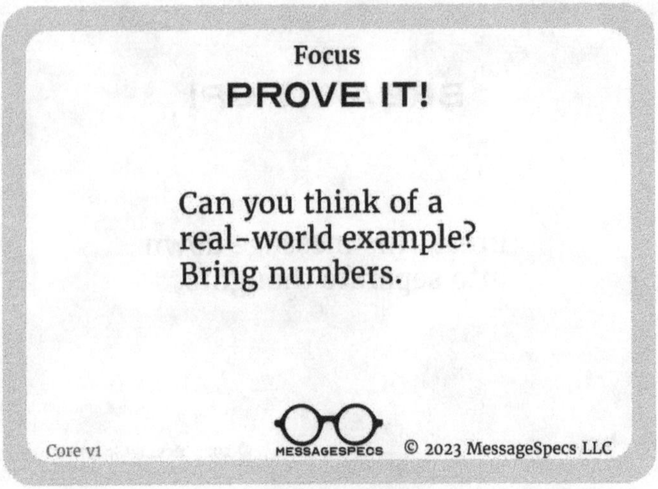

Focus
PROVE IT!

Can you think of a
real-world example?
Bring numbers.

Core v1   MESSAGESPECS   © 2023 MessageSpecs LLC

**Figure 61. Can you come up with ways to prove this?
(Hint: These can be related Proof Points!)**

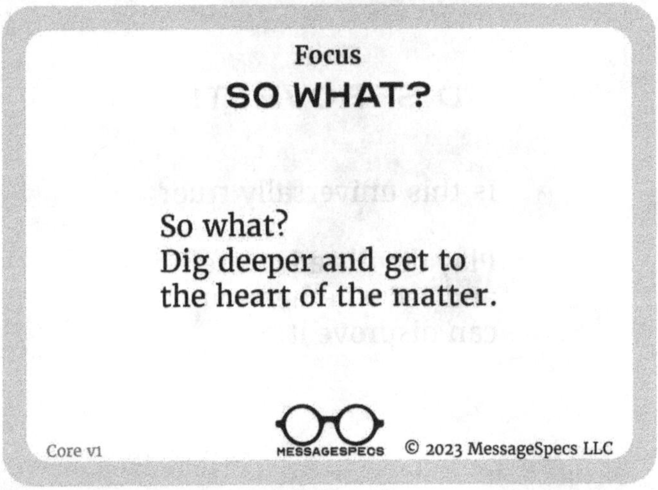

Focus
SO WHAT?

So what?
Dig deeper and get to
the heart of the matter.

Core v1   MESSAGESPECS   © 2023 MessageSpecs LLC

Figure 62. Why is this important? Or why did you say this?

Focus

STRIP IT!

Remove any technical
terms or jargon from
this card.
(Yes, even that one
term you really love.)

Core v1   MESSAGESPECS   © 2023 MessageSpecs LLC

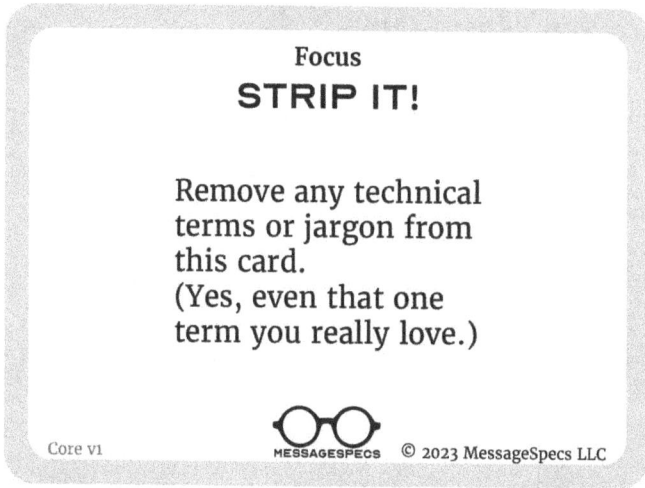

**Figure 63. My favorite to throw onto a Big Idea!
If you can't say what you want without the jargon,
you don't really know what you're talking about.**

These are all questions I've found myself asking the companies I've worked with time and again. They're nonconfrontational and allow you to gently nudge your participants (or yourself) with the quiet inner voice of a consultant.

It helps to have several of these prompts "in the bag," as it were, to pull out as a check on your first instinctive responses.

Before We Move On:

Put your therapist or consultant hat on for a moment.

What other "reverse" card questions can you come up with to prepare for your message workshop?

Consider all the little challenges and doubts that come to mind that you keep to yourself.

Think about objections that occur regularly in discussions with outsiders.

13

Cheesecake and Lunch Combos

How Options Enable Choice and Consistency

"Waitressing at the Cheesecake Factory is a complex socioeconomic activity that requires a great deal of analysis and planning. Bazinga!"

Sheldon Cooper
Former senior theoretical particle physicist at the California Institute of Technology and fictional character on *The Big Bang Theory*

∽◯◯∽

With outposts at suburban shopping malls across North America is a chain restaurant that has been called both "The Weirdest Restaurant On

Earth"[81] and "a marvel."[82] Founded in 1972, The Cheesecake Factory began as one son's tribute to his mother's humble bakery and has grown to over 300 locations worldwide.

Following an expansion in the 1990s, the chain's menu grew to over 20 pages and included more than 250 items at some locations. Flipping through the menu, you'll encounter a plethora of 29 categories, from small plates and appetizers to flatbread pizzas and salads to sandwiches and entrees to drinks and, of course, desserts that include over a dozen cheesecake varieties.

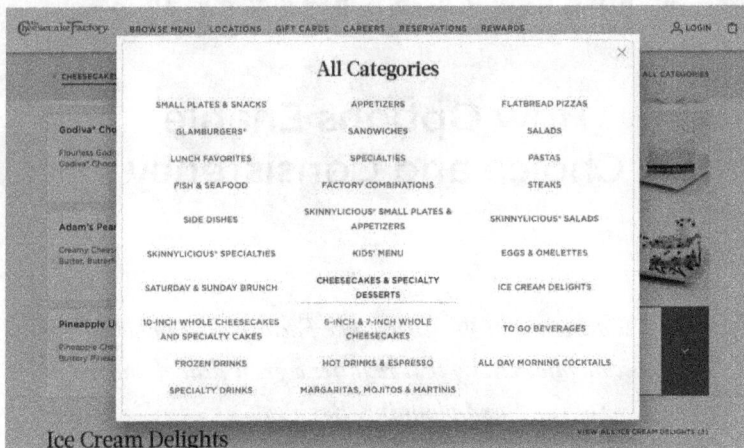

Figure 64. Screenshot of Cheesecake Factory menu. "Our Menu," The Cheesecake Factory, accessed January 26, 2025, https://www.thecheesecakefactory.com https://www.thecheesecakefactory.com/menu.

Frankly, it's enough to make one go a little cross-eyed when trying to decide. The genius part of The Cheesecake Factory, however, is that there's

---

[81] For a fun (and scathing look) at The Cheesecake Factory's design style, check out Robertas Lisickis, "Man Explains Why Cheesecake Factory Is Probably the Weirdest Restaurant on Earth and It's Pretty Spot On," Bored Panda, November 27, 2019, https://www.boredpanda.com/cheesecake-factory-restaurant-critic-tweet.

[82] Or, if you're more curious about how they pull off their menu, I recommend Alex Abad-Santos, "The Cheesecake Factory Knows What You Want," *Vox*, December 24, 2022, in.

almost nothing on the menu that's bad (personal food preferences aside).

Chasing Deliciousness

In a 2022 Vox Media article about the restaurant, journalist Alex Abad-Santos included a quote from Brandon Cook, The Cheesecake Factory's executive chef of culinary research and development. He said he hoped people thought of the chain as trying to bring whatever America wants to eat to its menu. Cook told Abad-Santos:

> So many other restaurant companies are driven by marketing departments, purchasing departments, and those are all necessary departments. But we're chasing deliciousness.[83]

Even with an abundance of varied offerings available, these "whatever America wants to eat" and "chasing deliciousness" concepts can certainly be seen as the unifying Big Idea behind the brand.

If The Cheesecake Factory can manage so many different offerings and show them together under one clear idea—then so can we!

Combos

How do we do it? Well, we've already discovered enough message options to create a Cheesecake Factory menu. Now it's time to see if we can bring the pieces together into a few "combos" that make sense.

Message combos put the different parts of a message together to focus its main idea for clarity on a specific audience or situation.

To do this, messages are framed through a few lenses, including:

- Audience

---

[83] Abad-Santos, "The Cheesecake Factory Knows What You Want."

- Outcome or Stage

- Medium

When considering these, use further prompts to shape the message. Some also have corresponding emotional, logical, and credibility aspects.

Audience Considerations

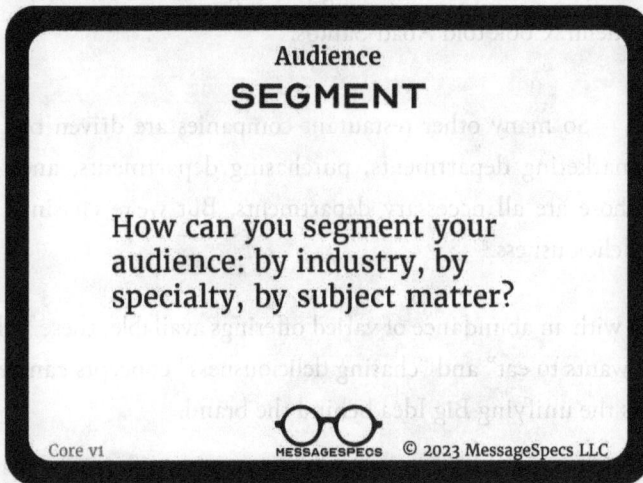

> **Audience**
> # SEGMENT
>
> How can you segment your audience: by industry, by specialty, by subject matter?
>
> Core v1   MESSAGESPECS   © 2023 MessageSpecs LLC

Figure 65. How to segment an audience? By industry, specialty, subject matter, role? Start by creating buckets of these and seeing how many different ways you can divide the audience.

Figure 66. Consider whether you can (and should) say the same thing to every role. What do they have in common? What sensitivities do they have?

This will help identify whether you can group or collapse audiences into larger sets. If you chase too many groups for which you can't use common messaging, you run the risk of appearing fractured.

A decent example of audience segmentation for a cybersecurity company could look like this:

- **By Industry:**

  Healthcare

  Financial Services

  Retail

  Education

  Government

- **By Specialty:**

  Network Security

  Application Security

Cloud Security

Incident Response

Compliance and Risk Management

- **By Subject Matter:**

Data Protection

Threat Detection

Vulnerability Management

Security Training

- **By Role:**

C-Suite Executives (CIO, CTO, CISO)

IT Managers

Security Analysts

Compliance Officers

DevOps Teams

You can further combine these. For example, regardless of industry or subject matter, all or most of these audience roles are concerned with data breaches, regulatory compliance, and maintaining customer trust.

They share a sensitivity toward cost-efficiency, the latest security trends, and solutions that can integrate seamlessly with their existing systems.

By recognizing these shared concerns, audiences can be grouped into larger sets like Decision-Makers (C-Suite, IT managers, etc.) and Implementers (security analysts, DevOps teams, etc.) for more streamlined messaging. So, start big and reduce.

You can also consider what information or motivation those audiences need to become advocates:

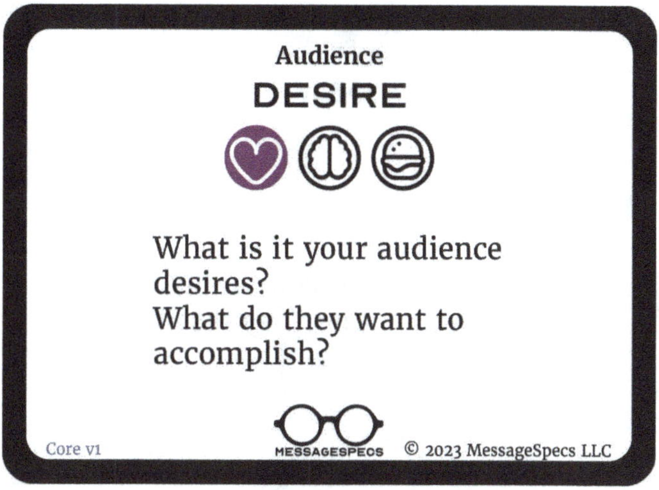

Audience

DESIRE

What is it your audience desires?
What do they want to accomplish?

Core v1 · MESSAGESPECS · © 2023 MessageSpecs LLC

Figure 67. What does the audience desire? What do they want or need to accomplish?

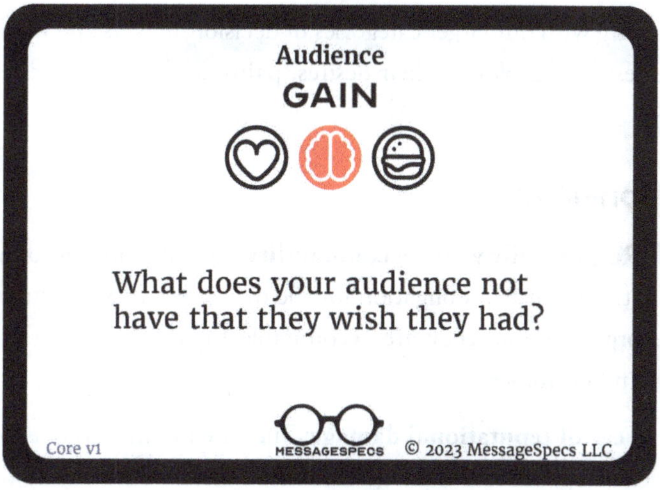

Audience

GAIN

What does your audience not have that they wish they had?

Core v1 · MESSAGESPECS · © 2023 MessageSpecs LLC

Figure 68. What does an audience not have that they wish they had? Pick just a few major ones.

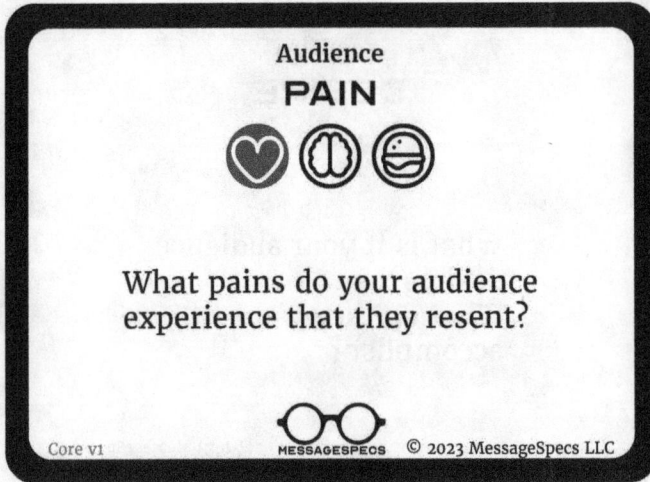

Figure 69. What pain points does the audience experience that they resent?

Sticking with our larger categories of decision-makers and implementers, the result of exploring their desires, pains, and gains could look like this:

Decision-Makers

- **Responsibility and accountability**: Decision-makers often feel a strong sense of obligation for the overall security posture of their organization. They are accountable to stakeholders, the board, and customers.

- **Fear of reputational damage**: They are highly sensitive to potential reputational damage that could arise from security breaches or noncompliance. This fear can drive a strong desire for reliable and trustworthy solutions.

- **Investment justification anxiety**: Decision-makers experience unease about justifying the cost of security investments to stakeholders and ensuring a return on investment (ROI).

- **Confidence and control**: They seek solutions that provide certainty over their organization's security environment. They need assurance that their decisions are the right ones.

Implementers

- **Stress and overwhelm**: Implementers often face anxiety due to the technical complexity of their work and the constant pressure to keep up with evolving threats and technologies.

- **Frustration with tools and processes**: They may be exasperated with security tools that are complex, difficult to use, or poorly integrated with existing systems.

- **Pride in expertise**: Implementers' self-worth is tied to their technical expertise and ability to protect the organization. They desire recognition for their skills and accomplishments.

- **Need for support and resources**: They require adequate training, resources, and support to perform their jobs effectively. The lack of these can lead to feelings of inadequacy or frustration.

Vitamins or Pain Relievers?

When considering pains versus gains in messaging, I always recommend putting pain first. The reason is that people are less likely to believe you can give them something they don't have. They're far more inclined to protect their state of well-being and remove the pain.

Outcome and Stage Considerations

To figure out how to connect messages to these audience views, you need to be clear about what you want from them right after sending a message. It also takes being realistic about outcomes. Do you want them to immediately say, "I need this" and write you a check after an initial demo? While that would be nice, it's also unlikely.

In chapter 7, we talked about how an audience needs different types of messages as they move through their journey. When you know who an audience is and what stage they are in, you can get the right information from the messaging system and use it correctly. But here's a reminder of what's typically most important as someone is transitioning between stages:

- **Unaware to aware**: Focus on emotional engagement with Big Ideas, Stories, and Values— introduce Mantras to create initial interest.

- **Aware to interested**: Maintain emotional connection while giving reminders of Big Ideas, introducing emotional and logical Value propositions, and building initial credibility through Proof Points.

- **Interested to evaluating**: Shift toward logical details with strong Value messages, extensive Proof Points, and Technicals that support evaluation.

- **Evaluating to committed**: Reinforce logical and credibility aspects with detailed Value propositions, Proof Points, and Technicals.

- **Committed to action**: Emphasize logical clarity and credibility to drive final decisions, supported by Technical details.

- **Action to advocate**: Foster emotional loyalty and community through Big Idea reminders, Stories, and Mantras—backed by ongoing Proof Points and Technical support.

Medium Considerations

How a message is presented is often as important (if not more so) than what you say. In 1964, Canadian communication theorist Marshall McLuhan coined the phrase, "The medium is the message."[84] By this, he was referring to how critical a delivery method can be to how a messages's meaning is interpreted or received.

We often call this the "channel" of the message. Whether you're

---

[84] Marshall McLuhan, *Understanding Media: The Extensions of Man* (McGraw Hill, 1964).

choosing a video medium (YouTube, Facebook Reels, or TikTok), a long-form text format (email newsletter, blog, white paper), or short-form text (social media post or paid advertisement), you need to keep in mind how much an audience can hold in theirs.[85]

I won't spend too much time on this—as there is no end to the number of expert guides out there on crafting a message based on your delivery method—but here are some considerations:[86]

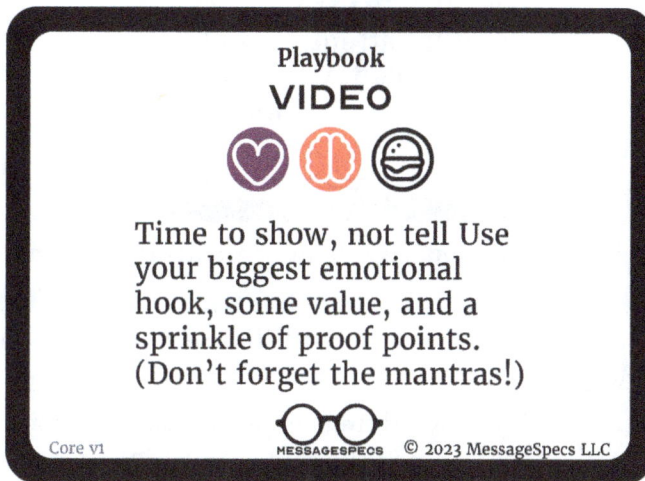

Figure 70. Video is hot now. So don't do it boring.

Video and audio media: It is crucial to harness the power of visual and auditory storytelling. These formats allow for delivering complex information in an engaging and accessible manner. They're also the closest to our base storytelling animal. So, use stories here as framing devices. Video design is especially important so that no more mental friction is introduced. For example, a spoken narration that doesn't follow the text on the screen can split the audience's focus. Additionally, incorporating subtitles and transcripts can enhance accessibility and broaden the audience's

---

[85] Back to the concept of the caveman mind from chapter 4.

[86] I'd suggest starting with McLuhan's seminal works *Understanding Media: The Extensions of Man* or *The Medium Is the Massage* (not a typo).

comprehension, taking some burden off their brains.

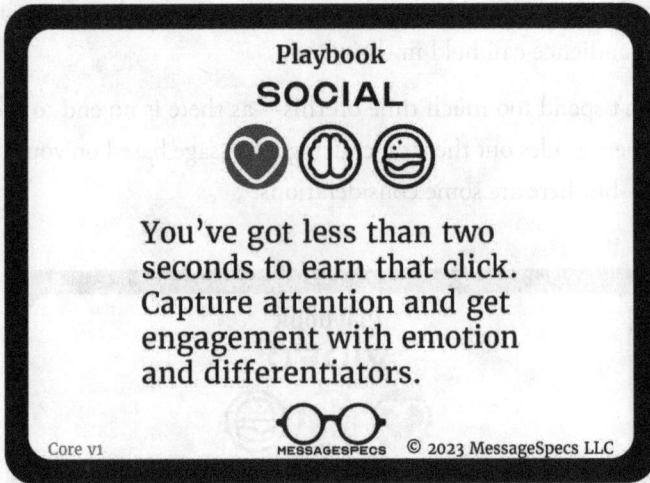

Figure 71. Social media is a game of moments, not minutes

Short-form text (social media and ads): These demand brevity and clarity. Each word must be carefully chosen to convey the message quickly and effectively. This medium thrives on catchy headlines, strong calls to action, and often visual elements to capture attention. The shorter the span of time you've got to get someone to read and click, the more emotional and jarring you should be. So, leverage the most emotional messages and lead them to deeper content.

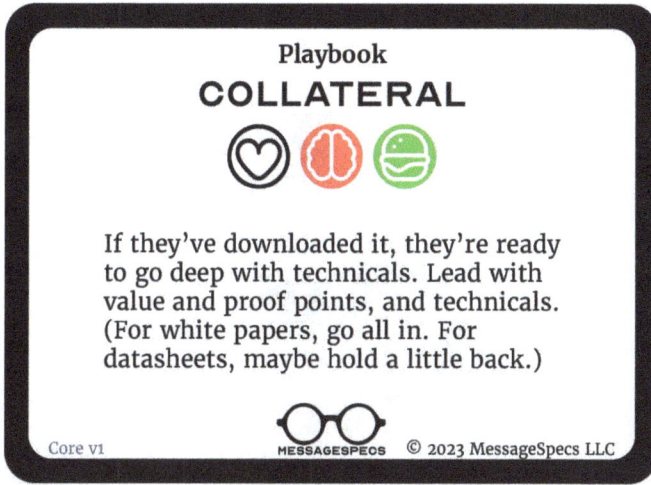

Figure 72. Geek out in longer form. But be balanced.

Longer-form text (blogs, white papers, and email newsletters): These allow for a deeper exploration of topics, providing an opportunity to establish thought leadership and convey complex ideas. But you also can't dump everything on an audience at once. When crafting blogs, white papers, and email newsletters, it's important to structure the content with clear headings, subheadings, and bullet points to enhance readability. Even with the most technical paper, it can help to integrate storytelling elements and case studies that can make the content more relatable and engaging.

This also goes for presenting slide decks. There's nothing more frustrating for an audience than the presenter reading a slide verbatim because the reading pace won't match their internal voice as they read along.

Rabbit Holes and Extra Credit

Advanced Strategies, Bonus Resources, and Other Stuff

I hope the first three parts have helped you understand how to make a good technical message. But no single book can cover everything. In case you want a little extra credit (and what nerd doesn't?), Part Four contains a few additional thoughts and perspectives that provide rabbit holes for you to go down.

These are side quests and other essays I've written that build on some of the basics in previous chapters. In the following pages, you'll find some tips on creating messaging systems for cross-organizational message adoption, scaling your messaging up for wider campaigns (or niching into a very small audience), and how to spot and avoid the typical marketing Big Idea.

14

Getting the Other Nerds on Board

What Good Is a Great Message if Nobody Uses It?

"A bad strategy will fail no matter how good your information is, and lame execution will stymie a good strategy."

Bill Gates
American businessman, investor, and philanthropist

〜

The sad truth about many branding and messaging engagements is that creatives put so much effort and energy into producing brands that look great but don't create useful content that communicates a tech solution.

Part of this is because communicators rarely have the resources to execute content and messaging well when it comes time to extend the "brand."

This was my experience, at least, as a content lead at an agency focused on serving tech companies.

After the brand blitz, our amazing designers created a PDF guide with imagery, look and feel mockups, style and tone of voice samples. We would include a grammar guide and some select taglines and slogans. Don't get me wrong, the guides were great for surface-level content or design work. But when the task came down to writing deep copy for a new website or planning a sustainable content campaign, there was rarely enough material to go on.

The result? The creatives would produce buzzword-bingo nonsense that would never pass a technical sniff test. Technical SMEs[87] and sales team members responsible for communicating on the front lines defaulted to oversharing and overloading—resulting in boring, pedestrian content.

That's where turning our Message Foundation into a Messaging System comes into play.

Creating a Messaging System

The objective of systematizing messaging is to go well beyond typical "voice and message guide" documents. Because audiences are dynamic and messaging evolves, a slide deck or document will never be able to keep up.

I recommend using a site that your entire organization can access and always use. This goes beyond sales or marketing.

Why? Because even internal staff—like the product team and developers—need to know how things are being presented to the rest of the world:

- What promises are being made to prospects that development will need to rise to?

- How are we inspiring the world to listen to our unique perspective and approach?

- What conversations are happening "out there?"

The bonus to creating a messaging system is that we nerds love

---

[87] Subject-Matter Experts

systems![88] If you can deliver messaging in a set of building blocks, and with enough context, it becomes easier for even non-creatives to adopt.

You can start with a simple spreadsheet like Microsoft Excel or Google Sheets and create a veritable menu of all messaging elements. The sheet could look something like this:[89]

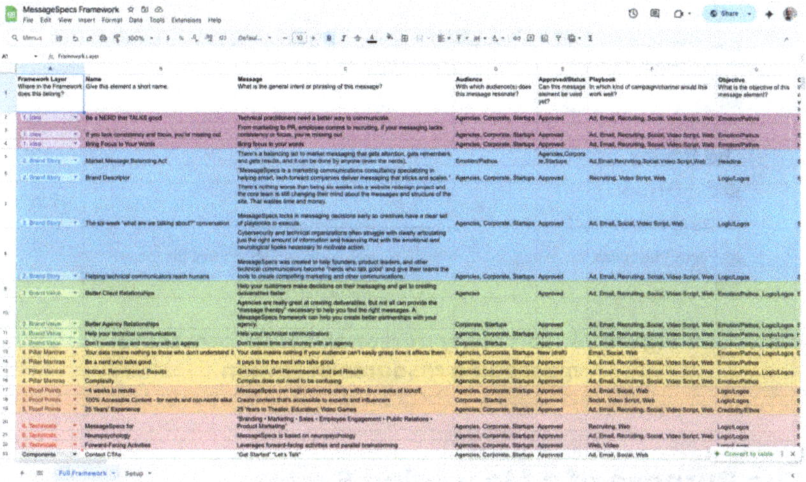

Figure 73. Messaging Framework in Google Sheets template

A spreadsheet can be a great starting point for seeing all the messaging options laid out before you.

But we can do *sooo much* better.

This needs to become the go-to messaging hub for the full company; it must be more useful and dynamic. I recommend using a flexible page builder like Notion, Airtable, or even Microsoft SharePoint as a "messaging hub."[90] Each has its own strengths and weaknesses, and whichever one is chosen will have a lot to do with what you have at your fingertips.

---

[88] Again, I know I'm not speaking for all nerds here. But, in general, highly technical people tend to be systems thinkers.

[89] If you want to see the full thing, you can copy the Prompts and Framework template from the Goodies page at nerdthattalksgood.com/goodies.

[90] Check out nerdthattalksgood.com/goodies to see some message system examples.

For the example below, I'll show you my own personal Notion template.

MessageSpec Library (Live)

> 💡 Welcome to your MessageSpecs Library!
>
> This is your living, breathing collection of your organizational truths and marketing messages. The more you and your team use it as both a source of reference and an organic repository of lessons learned, the stronger and more consistent your brand messaging will be!

The Basics
🍃 Content Catalog
👓 Clarity Framework
🎯 Focus Playbooks

Resources
⚗️ MessageSpecs Guide
🗒️ Content Central
🎹 Periodic Table of Bad Big Ideas
🐚 Brand Assets

Figure 74. This is my personal, living, breathing messaging resource in Notion.

The Purpose of a Messaging System

A messaging system goes far beyond just being a guidance document or even a style overview PDF. A messaging system should serve three purposes:

1. **Alignment and consistency**: This keeps everyone on the same page.

2. **Body of work**: A living, breathing source of what's working and what isn't.

3. **Validation and message pruning**: Provides a single source of truth on which to test new messaging.

Let's examine each of these individually.

Creating Alignment and Consistency

There are differing opinions within organizations about the most important messaging elements. Marketing often focuses on the top-level Big Ideas or Stories. Sales is all-in on Value Propositions and Proof Points. Customer success also focuses on Proof Points—but through the lens of the customer.

Naturally, this can result in groups focusing only on what's most relevant to their experience. This can leave audience members underinformed and underwhelmed.

Ensuring that each function in an organization is equipped with the same messaging elements means preparing everyone to seamlessly hand things off as appropriate. It also means that certain entities won't "go rogue" and begin making up messaging that conflicts with that of other groups.

A Body of Work

When I was head of content for a marketing agency, I would often be tasked with writing content for a client that I had not worked with before. Likewise, sometimes there would be an annual campaign—like a holiday or industry event—that we would be asked to replicate based on what we'd done previously.

In these circumstances, the team would scramble to scroll through months of Facebook, Twitter, and LinkedIn posts to figure out what the heck we had done before. Or the team would have a question about the meaning of a tagline or core message when the best resource we had to go on was the "creative brief" document that was written three years before the brand language had been finalized.

We had no access to case studies or examples of our best work.[91]

---

[91] Show me a marketing agency that does contemporaneous use cases and maintains an easily navigable body of work for their clients in one place and I'll buy you dinner the next time I see you!

Far beyond the typical "brand guide," a dynamic messaging system in Notion, SharePoint, or whatever, can become a place to upload examples of messaging in action.

Did a particular campaign message go viral in the marketplace or a slight tweak to a specific phrase get a big reaction? The messaging system is a place to drop in a link to content or screenshots. For example, after I added the Cluster-Thought Story to my system, I made a LinkedIn post about it. The Message System made it very easy to just drop in the link and artifacts of that post.

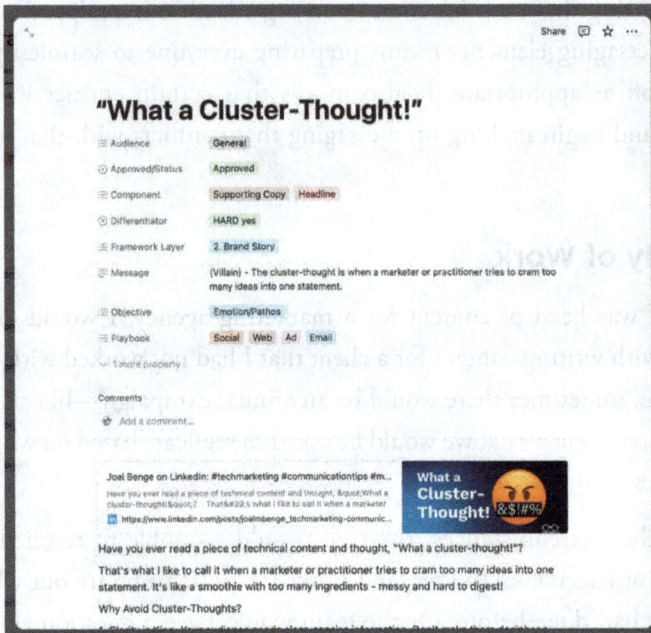

Figure 75. Entry for "villain" element (the Cluster-Thought)

Do you have multiple audiences, each of which needs to be presented with a targeted version of a core story? If so, capture clarity and include the specific version for the audience, where appropriate. Here, I've included three different versions of my top-level "nerd that talks good" message point—each customized for specific audiences.

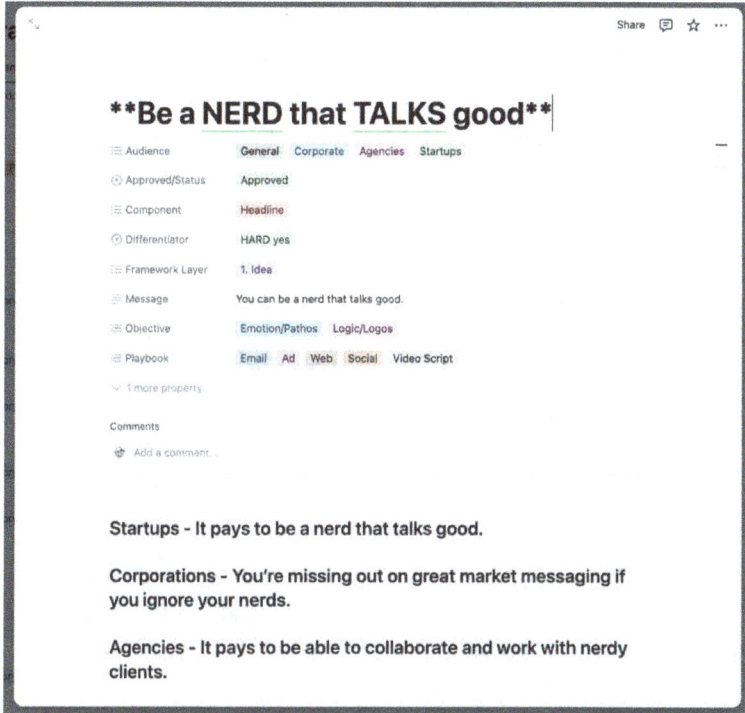

Figure 76. Notice that my Big Idea applies to corporations, agencies, and startups.

Message Validation and Pruning

Because messaging is dynamic—the market is always maturing and evolving, technologies evolve, and audiences move on—you want a messaging system that is flexible.

Rather than spend time reinventing the wheel at monthly or quarterly marketing and sales meetings—where you wonder what to focus on in the next period—use a message system to plan which core messages to table, and how to build on what you already have.

Your message system can be a resource to create a feedback loop for the organization. Staff can drop in comments or lessons learned "in the wild," which can be reviewed by the team at regular intervals to revise messaging.

Messages can also be tagged for status or classification. For example, I encourage clients to begin testing new messaging in small groups or limited campaigns. To track performance, they can add a messaging element to their system, but mark it as "draft" or "in development." This way, not everyone communicating on behalf of the company will use a message until it is approved.

Creating the System

This starts by importing all the output from workshop or messaging exercises into a database.

"A database? How nerdy!"

Yep!

Sourcing with a database or table view lets you introduce tagging, which speeds up messaging decision-making. It also allows you to create the playbooks for easier execution.

In my messaging system, I use the following tags and categories (but you can do whatever works for you):

- **Pyramid layer**: Obviously

- **Objective**: Emotion, logic, credibility

- **Target audience**: Does this message resonate with or need to be adapted for a specific audience?

- **Marketing element**: How does this element work best? As a headline, supporting statement, or call to action?

- **Differentiator**: Is this something only you can say? How defensible is it?

Automating Your Combos

Using a messaging system and labeling messages means quickly finding what you need with filters. In the systems I make for clients, I often include a simple picker that lets them create combos by choosing their audience, goal, and medium.

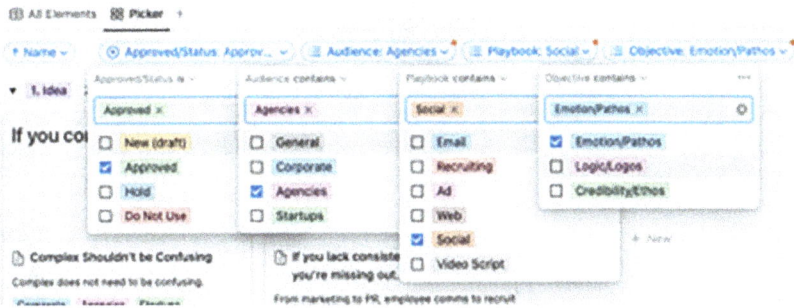

Figure 77. Message system picker using various filters

This lets anyone in the company quickly create a plan for managing weeks—or even months—of content tailored to their market needs that is always on message.

And if a spur-of-the-moment need comes up or someone in the company goes rogue and begins developing communication that's not in alignment, asking a few questions will help them find the right message and avoid wasted time and effort.

15

On Tailoring Messaging

From Off-the-Rack to Bespoke

"A tailor is a person's best friend as far as I'm concerned, because you can take things that fit OK or look OK, and if you get them tailored, they can be fabulous."

Betsy Hodges
American politician

The words "tailor" or "customize" appear in marketing quite often. What exactly does it mean to tailor a message? It seems counterintuitive that a book on developing core messaging is also advocating for the creation of unique pitches for each audience.

The trick is that if core messaging is developed well, you can take advantage of that foundation to create very targeted messages that make good on that clarity discussed in chapter 2. Knowing how far to take tailoring is a function of how replicable you want a message or campaign to be.

If you're just starting out, you may think all marketing is the same and any marketing firm or consultant can deliver. But just like buying an off-the-rack suit from a department store versus a one-of-a-kind garment from an artisanal professional, marketing comes in various levels of tailoring.

The bespoke option comes at a higher cost and lower scalability, but (generally) better quality messaging. Let's stick with clothing as a metaphor.

The Various "Grades" of Market Tailoring

Off-the-Rack, Ready-to-Wear

This level of marketing uses standard, mass-produced campaigns designed to reach a broad audience. These are typical, generic advertisements and social media posts not tailored to specific audience segments. The advantage is cost-efficiency and broad reach, but the downside is less relevance and personal connection with the audience. For this level of customization, you can easily rely on an AI marketing tool or inexperienced practitioner.

For Example: This is going to be most useful for reaching a broader audience on social media or as a paid ad campaign that is targeted at a nonspecific audience. These are also great for brand awareness, when you're just providing air cover for deeper messages.

Made-to-Measure

When adjusting strategy based on collected data such as demographics and general buying behaviors, you step up a level. Like adjusting a suit pattern, campaign approaches can be modified slightly to better fit the "measurements" of targeted market segments. This approach is more effective than off-the-rack because it considers an audience's general characteristics, though it's still based on preexisting templates. Expect to get this level of personalization from general creative and marketing agencies.

Custom, Personal Tailoring

More refined, offering deeper customization. It involves designing marketing strategies that are significantly more tailored to the specific needs of market segments. Here, you might choose specific platforms, content styles, and messages based on detailed analysis of audience behavior and preferences. There's more room for creativity and personalization, much like picking out specific fabrics and cuts in personal tailoring.

Bespoke

The highest level of customization that carefully matches the specific needs of each customer group or even each customer. Every element of custom marketing plans is crafted to order, from in-depth audience research to personalized messaging and channel strategies.

Bespoke marketing aims to engage at a personal level to create experiences and messages that resonate deeply and build strong brand loyalty. It often relies on in-house marketing teams experienced with your particular industry and audience. Some of the best marketers I know were once such practitioners and fit into this grade.

Haute Couture

We don't often see marketing on this level. But since it gives me an opportunity to pretend I am fancy and understand French, I'll go there. This level of marketing is like haute couture in fashion—exclusive, elaborate, and using the latest tech to create unique campaigns. This might involve immersive experiences like highly interactive and personalized digital platforms or extraordinary live events. It's not just marketing; it's an art form, designed to create a profound emotional impact and unforgettable experiences.

The money you're willing to spend and the impression you're trying to make are the two factors to consider when deciding how to dress—I mean market. For early-to-mid-stage startups, I generally see more focus on Made-to-Measure or Custom marketing. Once an organization gets large enough to support internal marketing efforts, they may step into Bespoke Marketing.

Notably, for very early-stage companies, Haute Couture marketing offers a unique opportunity to captivate a chosen few and create an exclusive circle of brand champions and pioneers. It's about investing in those highly personal, one-on-one connections with your very first supporters.

Before We Move On

Deciding on whether you need a closet full of clothes or just a capsule wardrobe[92] depends on how wide your audience is and how deep your pockets are. So think about:

What are your widest and most broadly-applicable messaging points that could apply and appeal to a big audience?

How different are your audience segments, really?

Can you "dress up" one basic message in a few different ways to suit them instead of developing new messages?

---

[92] A capsule wardrobe is a minimalist collection of clothing and accessories that can be mixed and matched to create a variety of outfits, focusing on essential, versatile pieces rather than trendy items.

16

The Periodic Table of Bad Big Ideas

Spotting and Avoiding Mistakes in Development

"Good order is the foundation of all good things."

Edmund Burke
Anglo-Irish statesman and philosopher

∽◯◯∽

Many companies resort to Big Idea clichés and tropes because they are so close to their product or solution that they regurgitate the Big Ideas seen elsewhere in the wild. This can even be driven by the unconscious mind.

I've worked with many clients and asked them what their Big Idea or differentiation was. They tell me something like "Our Technology—Your Success" or "Our People Make the Difference."

They think, "This feels really good!" or "It's totally us!" But a quick web search or some competitive research shows exactly how unoriginal and commonplace their phrasing is.

The reason it feels good is because there really are only a few Big Ideas out there. Being aware of them allows you to find a way to frame or shape what you want to say in a way that's truly original *and* authentic, while not falling into the trap of assuming you're the first team to come up with something.

Big Ideas Be Blowin' in the Wind

An occupational hazard of being a technical marketer is encountering bad Big Ideas in the wild at conferences like RSA or Black Hat. For those not in the cybersecurity field, these are the field's largest corporate events. Technology companies will spend hundreds of thousands of marketing dollars to get their messaging seen by attendees.

Sadly, some of the biggest companies default to the lamest, most clichéd tropes.

At a recent conference, I encountered more than one company whose biggest idea—no doubt one they paid hundreds of thousands of dollars for—was their being the "Global Leaders" in their competitive realm.

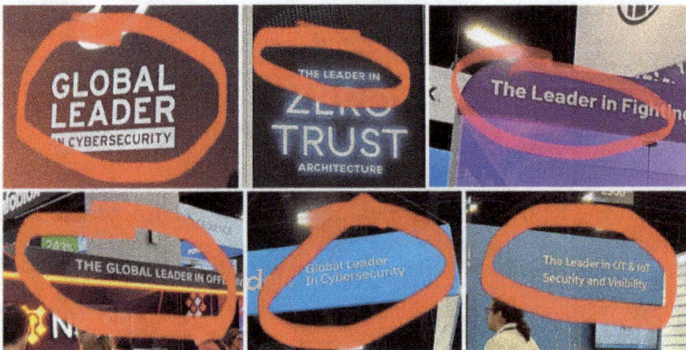

Figure 78. Follow the leader. Which one?

There were also many companies that wanted to help us take care of "what matters most" while completely leaving that up to interpretation.

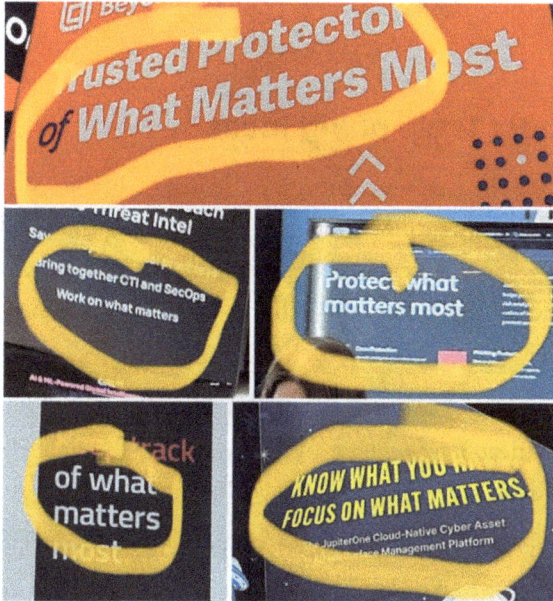

Figure 79. That's just, like uh, your opinion man.

Also popular among cybersecurity companies is the concept of control.

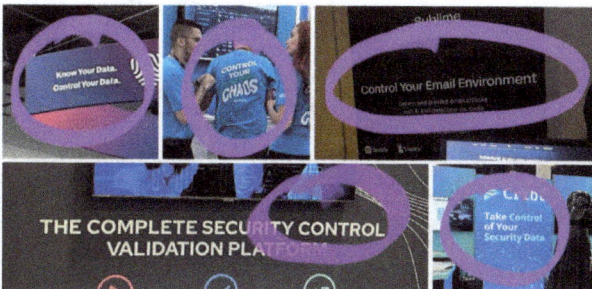

Figure 80. If the whole industry is crowing about control, it can feel very constricting.

I took to LinkedIn to vent about how cybersecurity marketers needed to *"stop copying each others' homework!"* and the post was met with over 150,000 impressions and hundreds of comments—primarily from cybersecurity buyers. If calling out an industry on their failure to message honestly and uniquely results in that level of reaction, we have a problem, Houston.

The Periodic Table of Big Ideas

The trick to avoiding this sameness is evaluating whether your Big Idea is solid, relatable, and familiar enough without falling into cliché territory. In science, we have references like the periodic table of elements to help categorize chemical compounds. What if we could do something similar for messaging?

After working with many companies over the years, I began to "collect" the Big Ideas I was seeing in the wild. This became the genesis of *another* card deck: *The Periodic Table of Big Ideas*.

This is my way of categorizing the underlying objectives and motivations behind most B2B or B2C brands. It represents the essence of a brand, broken down into its basic elements.

Big Ideas can be combined or bent to add nuance. But a good rule of thumb is to keep your Big Idea simple and avoid putting too many thoughts into it. Otherwise, it becomes the dreaded "cluster thought." You risk it being too niche or just plain bulky.

The Big Idea Families

There are 11 basic families (so far) in my Periodic Table, each with a very specific motivational thought or theme:

1. **Contrast**: Using differences to highlight unique features or benefits.

2. **Empathy**: Connecting on an emotional level by showing an understanding and care for the needs of customers.

3. **Empowerment**: Big Ideas that focus on enabling customers, highlighting how the brand enhances their capabilities or freedom.

4. **Expertise**: An emphasis on superior knowledge or skills in a specific area.

5. **Superiority**: Showcasing a leading position in the market, often through quality or innovation.

6. **Partnership**: Emphasizing collaboration and support for customers, creating a sense of allyship.

7. **Purpose**: Centered on mission or values that resonate on a deeper societal level.

8. **Scarcity**: Leveraging the classic marketing principle that limited availability increases desirability.

9. **Speed**: Highlighting quick service, rapid delivery, or efficiency.

10. **Versatility**: Flexibility or a wide range of uses or applications.

11. **Time**: Focuses on durability, heritage, or the time-saving aspect as the value proposition.

Transitional Big Ideas

Some Big Ideas can even be "transitional" and clearly fall into more than one family. And any Big Idea can be transmuted into another family unintentionally if the language or the sentence structure is tweaked. So, beware!

Objective Concentration

As a reminder, every Big Idea (and every element of messaging in general) is targeted to elicit one of three objectives—emotion, logic, and credibility.

A Big Idea that is highly aspirational, like *The Safe Choice*, or *Common Ground* will lean very emotional. Those like *Scale* and *Speed of Business* tend to appeal to logic, while those that leverage credentials like *The Pioneer* or *Heritage* will be more credibility-focused, and so on.

Big Ideas can appeal to more than one objective, depending on how they're expressed or their supporting ideas. However, they generally lean heavily toward a primary objective.

The Big Idea Elements

The Contrast Family

Cognitive Dissonance (Cd) [Emotion]: "We're [X], But We're Not [Y]"

Leverages contrast, especially against a status quo or stereotypical industry perception, taps into several psychological principles to capture attention, creates differentiation, and establishes a memorable brand identity:

- "We're smart, not stuffy."

- "Cold tech. Warm bodies."

- "We're specialists, not generalists."

Familiar Innovation (Fi) [Logic]: "The [X] of [Y]"

This uses familiar brands to clarify new ideas, quickly establish expectations, and build trust. It's like saying, "It's similar to something you already know, but for a different market":

- "We're the Waze of cybersecurity."

- "We're the Uber of farmers' markets."

- "We're the Airbnb of cloud service providers."

Holistic Value (Hv) [Logic]: "More Than What You Think"

"More than" is a powerful way to highlight the added value a brand provides beyond the expected or basic service. It explicitly draws a line between the ordinary and the extraordinary aspects of what the brand offers.

It can also emphasize emotional resonance or logical advantages, making it a versatile storytelling tool:

- "More than learning—unlocking your true potential."

- "Beyond strength: Building resilience for life."

- "Building businesses, not just networks."

Infomercial Alternatives (Ia) [Emotion]: "What's in your _____?"

The question subtly suggests that the alternatives may not be optimized or may not align with the audience's goals. This creates an implicit comparison with the status quo, encouraging individuals to think about potential improvement:

- "What's in your wallet?" (Made popular by Capital One.)

- "Who's watching over you?"

- "Who's in your network?"

- "Is your strategy holding you back?"

Intersection (Is) [Logic]: "At the Intersection of [X] and [Y]"

Similar to contrast, this approach tries to draw a connection between disparate thoughts, unifying them into a single hybrid:

- "At the intersection of technology and humanity."

- "Where business and fun meet."

- "At the crossroads of education and marketing."

The Empathy Family

Shared Journey (Sj) [Emotion]:
"We Feel Your Pain"

Demonstrates the empathy of "we've been in your shoes," so we are the best partner to solve your problems today:

- "At your back. By your side."

- "Walking the path together, every step of the way."

- "Empathy beyond metrics, compassion beyond transactions."

The Empowerment Family

Behind the Scenes (Bs) [Logic]:
"The power behind the product"

Demonstrates that the brand doesn't manufacture end-user products or services; instead, it contributes essential components and expertise to improve and empower those provided by other companies:

- "We don't make the products you buy. We make the products you buy better." (Made popular by BASF.)

- "Enhancing the core of your business software for maximum impact."

- "Your secret weapon for business excellence."

Efficiency (Ef) [Logic]:
"Do More [X] with Less [Y]"

Communicates a commitment to efficiency, resource optimization, and achieving superior outcomes with minimal input. It appeals to businesses looking to maximize impact while conserving resources:

- "Maximize impact, minimize resources."

- "Do more. Waste nothing."

- "Optimize operations, amplify results."

The Driver's Seat (Ds) [Emotion]: "Take Control"

The psychology here is leveraging fundamental human needs and desires, including empowerment, security, mastery, and positively framing challenges:

- "Take control of your security data."

- "Total control of your network."

- "Control at your command."

- "Control your chaos."

The GPS (G) [Emotion]: "Where Are You Going?"

Inspires individuals and businesses to dream big, explore uncharted territories, and embrace the infinite possibilities that await them. Each slogan encourages the audience to push boundaries and envision a future full of achievement and success:

- "How far will you go?"

- "Go farther. Get more."

- "Where can we take you?"

- "Wherever your business takes you."

Turn the Tables (Tt) [Emotion]: "Stop [X] Before [X] Stops You"

Positions the consumer as the conqueror or survivor in the face of an adversary. Paints a clear "after" image of the user as a hero in a moment of triumph. But it also hints at a darker potential alternative outcome without the product:

- "Swat mosquitoes before they bite."

- "Outpace risks."

- "Flip doubt on its head."

- Anything with the concept of "hack back."

Unleash (U) [Emotion]: "Unleash Your [X]"

The concept of "unleash" suggests freeing up potential or capabilities perhaps currently constrained or not fully realized. It embodies a sense of empowerment and liberation. Can be framed around the notion that everyone has inherent excellence or potential that they can tap into with the right tools, guidance, or environment provided by the brand:

- "Unleash your excellence."

- "Discover your inner expertise."

- "Leave limits behind."

The Expertise Family

Heritage (H) [Credibility]: "We Paved the Way"

Emphasizes the brand's journey and growth, highlighting its evolution from one industry to another while maintaining a focus on innovation and leadership in the current industry:

- "We come from [X]. That's how we know [Y]."

- "From [X] pioneers to [Y] innovators."

- "Roots in [X], visionaries in [Y]."

- "Trailblazing [X], redefining [Y]."

More (Mr) [Credibility]:
"Nobody Does It Better"

Emphasizes the brand's unmatched commitment and proficiency in a specific area. Demonstrates a high level of successful engagements or customers:

- "When it comes to [X], we set the bar."

- "Nobody does more [X] than we do."

- "Thousands of successes strong."

The Benchmark (B) [Logic]:
"Purpose-Built"

Expertise in this context is about demonstrating a deep understanding of user needs and industry demands, resulting in products or services that are tailor-made to address specific challenges or enhance certain activities:

- "Purpose-built to do [THING]."

- "Made for humans. Built to connect."

The Pioneer (Pr) [Credibility]:
"The 'OG' Brand"

Emphasizing a brand as "The Original" taps into themes of authenticity, legacy, and pioneering spirit. It can also convey that the brand has empowered an entire industry or market through its innovations:

- "We built the original. Now we've made it better."

- "In [Year], we started a revolution. Today, we continue to lead."[93]

- "Decades of innovation."

- "Pioneering excellence since [YEAR]."

---

[93] This Big Idea can also be cross-referenced within the Time Traveler (Td) element, because it has a sort of "yesterday vs. today" concept. I told you some of these could be slippery.

The Safe Choice (Sc) [Emotion]:
"Prioritizing Trust"

Underscores the importance of trust and reliability in business relationships, particularly in the context of technology purchases. It acknowledges that decision-makers often prioritize established and reputable brands to minimize the risk associated with significant business investments:

- "Nobody ever got fired for buying IBM." (Made popular by some computer company whose name escapes me at the moment.)
- "Tomorrow's assurance, today's choice."
- "The trusted choice."
- "The global market leader in …"

The Partnership Family

Common Ground (Cg) [Emotion]:
"We Get You"

A strategic and empathetic approach aiming to establish a deep connection with B2B clients. It leverages shared experiences to build credibility and trust:

- "We know your world."
- "We've been in your shoes."
- "Work with a partner that understands your business like you do."

Force Multiplier (Fm) [Logic]:
"Amplifying Customer Success"

Centers on positioning the brand not merely as a service provider, but as an indispensable ally in the journey to success. It emphasizes the brand's role in significantly enhancing the capabilities and outcomes of its clients' businesses:

- "Our technology. Your success."

- "More than solutions: We multiply your wins."

- "Beyond solutions: Unleash the power of partnership."

Partnership (P) [Emotion]: "Taking Care of the Small Stuff"

Leverages psychological elements such as stress relief, confidence, and a sense of freedom to focus on core competencies and not the burdens of the solution provider's problem:

- "We do [X] so you can focus on [Y]."

- "You focus on your business. We'll handle the [X]."

- "Security solved, so you can get back to business."

The Purpose Family

Mission-Oriented (Mo) [Emotion]: "Mission-Oriented"

Assures the audience that there are no alternative motives or objectives hiding in the business relationship. This is often used on government audiences to co-opt the audience's mission statements:

- "Our mission is your mission."

- "We're here to support your mission."

- "Our only mission is yours."

What Matters (Wm) [Emotion]: "Whatever Matters to You"

The simplicity and versatility of this concept make it applicable to a wide range of security-related products or services. It can resonate with both B2B and B2C audiences. But it is nonspecific and puts the burden on the audience to complete the thought:

- "Do what you need. We do the rest."

- "Where it counts."

- "Secure What Matters."[94]

The Scarcity Family

FOMO (Fo) [Emotion]: "Don't Get Left Behind"

Focuses on the unknown or fear of missing out because of inferior products and services:

- "Settling for standard?"

- "Don't let limitations hold you back."

- "Don't let unexpected expenses derail your plans."

Optimization (O) [Logic]: "More with Less"

Leveraging the principle of scarcity promotes the brand's solutions as essential for maximizing limited resources, such as time, money, or materials. It appeals to businesses that need to perform optimally within constrained environments:

- "Make every resource count."

- "Optimize everything."

- "Get more with less."

---

[94] This was one of the early Big Ideas behind my startup, and I always chuckle when I see another company using it.

Scarcity (Sy) [Emotion]: "Overcoming Constraints"

Focusing on scarcity related to resource constraints, such as limited talent or shrinking budgets, to position a brand as a vital solution in times of need or efficiency. This approach not only acknowledges the challenges faced by potential clients but also highlights the brand's relevance and utility under such conditions:

- "Maximize potential, even when resources aren't at their max."

- "Stretch your budget, not your credibility."

- "You don't have time to save time. But we can."

The Speed Family

Mission Speed (Ms) [Emotion]: "Mission Never Stops"

Focuses not just on speed in general, but on speed as it pertains to accomplishing specific goals or missions. This concept emphasizes the efficiency and effectiveness with which a business can achieve targeted outcomes, making it particularly relevant for sectors where timing is critical to success:

- "Your timeline. Our commitment."

- "Your mission can't wait."

- "Your mission. On time."

Speed of Business (Sb) [Emotion]: "Taking Care of Business"

Emphasizes agility, responsiveness, and the ability to keep pace with the ever-changing demands of the business landscape. Promotes the brand as helping clients stay ahead without missing a beat:

- "Data at the speed of business."

171

- "Your finances, on your time."

- "Business moves fast. So can you."

The Superiority Family

Exclusivity (Ex) [Emotion]:
"We're the Only [X] That [Y]s"

Focuses on the brand's unique features or services not available anywhere else, enhancing its market position as superior and exclusive:

- "We're the only platform that adapts to your habits."

- "We're the only brand that crafts with authentic Martian leather."

- "We're the only snack made with Himalayan pink salt harvested under a full moon."

FIRST! – (F) [Logic]:
"Paving the Way"

Emphasizes the brand's commitment to leading the way in innovation, breaking new ground, and setting standards that others follow. Highlights the brand's role as an innovator and leader by being the first to introduce a new product, service, or approach in the industry:

- "Create first, inspire always."

- "First in innovation, foremost in impact."

- "Where innovation leads, success follows."

Scale (Sl) [Logic]:
"Bigger. Faster. Stronger. More."

Scale highlights the expansive capabilities and robustness of a brand. It can symbolize not only size but also the adaptability and reach of a brand's operations, products, or services:

- "Magnify your expectations."

- "Worldwide. Anytime. Anywhere."

- "From local to global, your trusted partner."

Simpler (Si) [Emotion]: "Keep It Simple, Smarty"

Indicates that a simpler approach results in superior outcomes, distinguishing it from competitors that may offer more complex solutions:

- "Simply versatile."

- "Simplicity wins every time."

- "Simply tech. Simply better."

The Time Family

Preventive Action (Pa) [Logic]: "No Surprises"

Emphasizes the proactive, preventive, and forward-thinking nature of a brand. This concept can be particularly compelling in industries where anticipation and prevention of problems are crucial, such as cybersecurity, healthcare, insurance, or risk management:

- "Stop attacks before they happen."

- "Future-proof your today."

- "See around the corner." (This was another tagline my startup used back in 2016ish.)

- "Fix it before it fails."

Time Travelers (Td) [Emotion]: "Today and Tomorrow"

Effectively uses the concept of today versus tomorrow to show how immediate decisions or actions lead to significant future benefits, creating a compelling narrative around the impact of choosing the right brand or product. Can take the conceptual perspective of standing in the present and looking into the future, thereby keeping a foot in the past, present, or future (or any combination) or living in the future and looking back:

- "Where now meets next."

- "Building your tomorrow today."

- "Today's technology. Tomorrow's needs."

The Versatility Family

David and Goliath (Dg) [Logic]: "Bigs vs. Smalls"

By merging the best of both worlds, promises clients and customers the efficiency and reliability of a large company with the intimate customer service and local expertise of a small one. This approach is particularly appealing to those who value both robust support and individual attention:

- "Local heart, global reach."

- "From the boardroom to your living room."

- "Big scale, small feel."

Tailored Solutions (Ts) [Logic]: "Tailored Solutions"

Showcases a unique capability to handle projects and clients of any size, from sprawling enterprises to small startups. Emphasizes adaptability and commitment to providing customized solutions that meet the needs of every client, regardless of scale:

- "Big or small. We do it all."

- "Flexibility at any scale: Customized for you."

- "Scaling to your needs, whatever they are."

Wrapping Up

Make it through all of those to see if your Big Idea was in there? I applaud you. If that Big Idea you thought was brilliantly original was listed, my condolences.

But take heart. That doesn't mean you shouldn't—and can't—use it. The Periodic Table is here as a reminder that there really are no "original" ideas—only original(ish) ways to present them.

Use these Big Ideas as inspiration or to gauge what resonates, then do a little further searching to find your own unique twist.

17

Masters of the Messaging Universe

How to Talk Tech Like He-Man

"If you're gonna lead the life of an adventurer, you might wanna keep a journal. Write down everything you ever do, even the silly stuff that you think is forgettable. Because when the adventures are over, that's all you're left with: good friends and happy memories."

Orko the Great
Cartoon magician and comic-relief from *He-Man and the Masters of the Universe* franchise

*(Note: This chapter was originally a blog post for my first creative
agency when the message model was just forming in my brain.
It has been updated very slightly to align terminology.[95])*

Let's take a walk down memory lane and look at five lessons to message your tech like He-Man and the Masters of the Universe.

Three days after my seventh birthday, I witnessed the most compelling commercial ever, one that offered a product that would change my life—or at least my Saturday mornings—for the next three years.

It was a 30-minute animated production (with its own meta-commercial breaks) for a series of toys by Mattel—He-Man and the Masters of the Universe. That product franchise would create over $2 billion in revenue for Mattel over the next several years.

Who *wouldn't* love $2 billion built on marketing?

---

[95] Read the original here: adgcreative.net/resources/market-your-product-like-he-man. Thanks to ADG for letting me use it and their talented graphic designer for the sweet graphics.

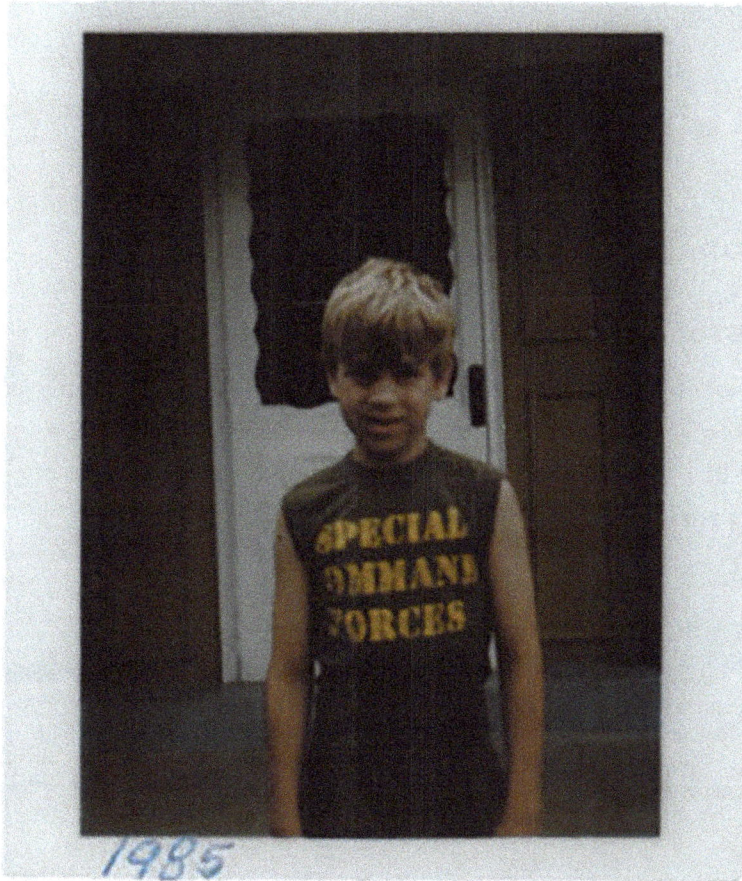

**Figure 81. Me at peak He-Man influence
(age 9)**

Five things Mattel did that you can do

1. The Big Idea

According to self-described He-Man inventor and former Mattel designer Roger Sweet, the pitch that got He-Man made was simple. Sweet knew that if he gave marketing something they could easily sell, he would jump ahead of the crowd. He chronicled this in his 2005 book, *Mastering the*

Universe: He-Man and the Rise and Fall of a Billion-Dollar Idea:

> *I simply explained that this was a powerful figure that could be taken anywhere and dropped into any context because he had a generic name: He-Man!*[96]

The Big Idea that sold Mattel on investing millions into creating the He-Man lineup was dead simple.

Lesson 1: Simplify Your Introduction

When the human brain encounters something new, it cannot easily retain a list of features or facts. Simple categorization at first impression is key. The best you can hope for is the audience walking away with one Big Idea for a product, like "they are an X for a Y."

Think About This

We've already covered Big Ideas earlier in this book. But how you introduce them is just as important. What are some ways that you can streamline introducing your idea to captivate attention and leave no room for confusion?

The more descriptive you are while remaining less specific, the more room for deeper explanations later—and you won't turn off the audience before getting there.

For a tech product, reconsider the urge to introduce yourself as an "end-to-end encryption solution for small business emails with Brownian motion-based hybrid symbol substitution and symbol interleaving for encryption keys." Instead, tell them you provide "business communications with physics-based encryption."

2. Bigger, Badder, Buffer

Before He-Man toys were introduced, the industry-standard action figure was three-and-a-half inches tall. *Star Wars* and G.I. Joe represent the best

---

[96] Roger Sweet and David Wecker, *Mastering the Universe He-Man and the Rise and Fall of a Billion-Dollar Idea* (Emmis Books, 2005).

examples.[97] The toys typically stood straight at attention in stiff poses.

When designer Sweet first envisioned He-Man, he took an existing Mattel action figure in the larger six-inch range and added massive clay muscles. Eventually, he developed the prototypical He-Man model—barrel-chested, knees bent in a horse stance, arms akimbo—that became the signature for most He-Man figures.

Figure 82. Puny Star Wars figures vs. the mighty He-Man!

Toys with this new "action" stance stood up on their own and were more rugged to play with. Again, Sweet followed through on his simple introduction with a product that was simply better.

Compare He-Man to the figures that came before it and he most definitely stands out. Following the success of He-Man, more toys followed suit and five-and-a-half inches became the new industry standard. The Teenage Mutant Ninja Turtles line that followed in 1990 definitely took a lesson from Sweet's product design, and soon dominated the marketplace—eventually displacing He-Man.

Lesson 2: Differentiate to Disrupt

Find opportunities for a product to look and sound different than those of competitors. If you can describe a product but substitute your brand name

---

[97] Yes, the original G.I. Joes of the 1960s were 12-inches, but by the time I was playing with them in the 1980s, we had the shorty versions.

with one of theirs—and the description is even 80% accurate—you stand the chance of being seen as an "also-ran." Change the description until your product is the only one that works.

Differentiation should also be rooted in the brand's Big Idea. Find whatever makes you different and expand on that. And be prepared to explain and defend it as a conscious decision.

What's Your WOW?"

A good rule of thumb while you're collecting your messaging elements and building your messaging system is to tag them according to their differentiation.

Hard Yes: This is a clear, unique advantage that directly addresses a specific need or desire of your audience. It's undeniable, easy to understand, and valuable to your target market. For example, "Our laptop is the lightest and fastest in the market for professionals who travel frequently." It's a differentiator that makes customers go, "I need that!"

Soft Yes: This is a differentiator that might be useful or appealing, but it's not unique or compelling enough to win customers on its own. It might overlap with what competitors offer or be less directly aligned with the audience's needs. For example, "We offer customizable color options for our laptop." It's nice but not necessarily a dealmaker.

No: This isn't really a differentiator—it's either too generic, not relevant, or something competitors also provide. For example, "Our laptop comes with a keyboard." It's a baseline expectation rather than a standout feature, so it doesn't influence buying decisions.

The distinction often boils down to whether the differentiator truly solves a problem, fills a gap, or delivers exceptional value compared to others.

Before We Move On:

Is your differentiation connected to your Big Idea or an add-on?

Look at all of your major messaging points and note whether they are a Hard Yes, Soft Yes, or No. Find the Hard Yes ones and see if you can weave them into the Big Idea.

3. The He-Man Bible

While the toys were a hit from the start, there was no context for the characters. According to screenwriter Michael Halperin, Mattel "… would get phone calls and letters from parents of kids who had purchased the toys. And they didn't know who were the good guys and who were the bad guys."[98]

In fact, they tried to include a comic book with the early figures, but the origin stories were confusing and did not align with one another. There was no cohesion of context.

This is why Mattel engaged the animation studio Filmation to create the first toy-to-show tie-in. The first thing Mattel did to prepare the Masters of the Universe series was develop a series bible.[99] This document laid the foundation for every storyline and character in the universe, outlining the history, locations, characters, and themes of the series—providing this clear reference:

> He-Man fights a never-ending war to wipe out evil
> from Eternia and ensure that goodness, purity, and virtue
> reign supreme throughout the universe!

No subsequent story was produced that wasn't checked against the bible.

Lesson 3: Be Consistent to Provide Context

Consider a series bible the organizational equivalent of your messaging system, including your brand guides. I know branding is often the last thing

---

[98] Jamie Greene, "A Thorough Oral History of He-Man and The Masters Of The Universe, The Game-Changing '80s Toon," SyFy, January 14, 2019, https://www.syfy.com/syfy-wire/a-thorough-oral-history-of-he-man-and-the-masters-of-the-universe-the-game-changing-80s.

[99] Thanks to the fandom and intrepid internet archivists, you can read it at "Masters of the Universe Bible," Wiki Grayskull, https://he-man.fandom.com/wiki/Masters_of_the_Universe_Bible.

on the minds of technical entrepreneurs. However, without a clear (and widely adopted) source of truth and body of work, sales and product teams may not be on the same page. Worse yet, the market will have no clear context to understand your product because, depending on the individual delivering the message, they will hear a different story.

Invest in a solid messaging foundation and find a good branding and marketing partner to help tell your story and get the entire team on board. Make your messaging the bible that holds the company together and gives it personality.

4. You Have the Power!

Any good product marketer knows the mantra "People don't buy features, they buy solutions to problems." But even the best entrepreneurs sometimes fail to do this.

Imagine how most tech companies today might introduce a product like He-Man—with a PowerPoint slide:

WHO IS HE-MAN?

- He-Man stands five-and-a-half inches tall.

- He has six points of articulation, including the shoulders, head, and a rubber-band that facilitates movement in the legs and waist.

- He-Man comes equipped with three accessories—a sword, axe, and shield—which are attached to a breastplate.

- He-Man figures come attached to an eight-inch info-card with supporting documentation.

Figure 83. No ... more ... POWERPOINT!

"Wow," I can hear you exclaiming. "Shut up and take my money!" ... Not.

This is not the sales presentation that made so many of my peers and me drool into our bowls of Trix and Lucky Charms (or Raisin Bran, in my case … thanks Mom) on Saturday mornings.

Instead, here is how eight-year-old me saw He-Man:

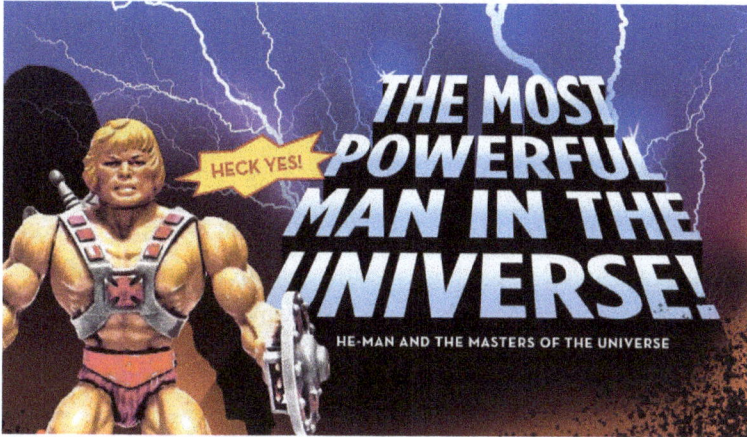

Figure 84. Heck yes!

The television commercials (not the cartoons) were chock-full of second-person imagery, which put me squarely into the story they were telling and made me want to experience it for myself.

It's All About the Power

> "YOU can pit He-Man against Beast-Man, playing for the POWER of Castle Grayskull!"

> "YOU have the power!"

They showed kids and their parents (usually a dad) playing with the characters in a living room. Invariably, the "storyline" involved the dad playing the "bad guys" with the kids playing the "good guys"—using their rubber-band-powered punch action or other gimmicks to knock over the bad guys and "win" the conflict.

The message was clear, "He-Man characters let you be the hero." That sort of sales pitch was (and still is) undeniable to an eight-year-old or a C-suite executive.

Lesson 4: Sell a Vision of the Consumer, Not Product Features

No executive is looking at the mountains of problems and work they have and longing for another piece of technology. They are looking to be delivered from headaches and heartaches they face every day. More than that, however, they want to be the hero.

Putting consumers front and center as potential heroes is a surefire way to get their attention. A good introduction and deeper dive into this topic is *Building a StoryBrand* by Donald Miller, which provides a basic model of this approach in marketing. But there are many other ways to tell a story than simply the Hero's Journey.

Marketing is not about you or your technology. It's about telling your audience a story about them and what they can be via you or your technology.

Before We Move On:

> What other stories can you tell your audience about their experience that aren't just the typical "we'll make you stronger, better, etc." ones?

Head back to chapter 8 if you need a refresher on Stories.

5. Cartoons, Lunchboxes, and Movies, Oh My!

When the Masters of the Universe figures were first brought to market—before the television series—success was marginal, though they were successful enough that Mattel realized it had something different that had potential. The challenge was boosting its signal to rise above the noise of *G.I. Joe* and *Star Wars*.

The obvious tactic was to launch a television series. While doing so, Mattel abandoned its comic books and partnered with DC Comics to insert mini He-Man comics into their existing titles. After all, why market to those who have already purchased your product?

Mattel also made every effort to get their brand exposed to as many passive eyes as possible—not all of whom were looking to buy an action figure at that moment, but might later. This took the form of brand placement on lunchboxes, bedsheets, View-Master reels (sort of like a 1980s Meta Quest), notebooks, stickers, Shrinky Dinks (Google those), coin banks, and lots and lots of other merchandise.

Figure 85. If you're not eating lunch out of these, really, are you eating though?

Eventually, they made a live-action movie with Dolph Lundgren,[100] the inimitable Frank Langella, and Courtney Cox in only her second credited movie role.

---

[100] This movie currently has a 21% rating on Rotten Tomatoes, https://www.rottentomatoes.com/m/masters_of_the_universe. (We no longer speak about that film. Not every channel was ready for He-Man, which is a shame, really.)

Lesson 5: Go Multichannel and Multi-Touch

We call what Mattel did "content marketing." The purpose is not to sell a product directly, but to elevate a brand's status in the marketplace. This is done through thought leadership (writing on blogs or in print media, engaging with the market through social media and other public campaigns), and producing content that adds value to the audience experience.

Stuck on Repeat

Marketing psychologists have agreed that people generally need to hear something five to seven times before it sticks and they take action on it. But that doesn't mean you need to deliver the same talking point or message verbatim each time.

For example, there are only a handful of messages I repeat:
- Balance Heart, Head, and Gut messaging.
- Get noticed, get remembered, and get results.
- Create messaging that stands out, sticks, and scales.
- Design communication that connects deeply, persuades smartly, and lasts forever.
- Hook them emotionally, prove your value, and leave them wanting more.
- Balance feeling, thinking, and believing to amplify your message.

Each of these messages has the same core structure of thought. (Bonus if you spot the Rule of Three.) By using these messages repeatedly, my objective is to come at the audience with the same core message using a multi-touch approach

Consistent, but subtly-varied messaging keeps a brand "top of mind" and needs to be done via many different channels. This multichannel, high-touch approach ensures that when a prospect is ready to seek a solution, yours is the one they turn to.

Before We Move On:

If you have a grasp on what your core messaging points are, see if you can come up with alternate ways to phrase them that echo the clarity of intent but place the focus on different aspects.

Generative AI tools like ChatGPT or Gemini can also be useful in rephrasing, but don't just regurgitate what they spit out. Be critical.

Knowing Is Half the Battle

(Okay, so that's *G.I. Joe*, but go with me on this.)

Every He-Man episode ended with a moral, so I'll follow suit.

Today's consumer has about the same attention span as a 1980s eight-year-old. That's not necessarily a bad thing, but we need to market to them accordingly:

- **Simplify the introduction**: Just because you're selling a highly technical product doesn't mean sales collateral should be at a PhD level.

- **Be different to disrupt**: You can't stand out in the market if you look like everyone else. Find a niche or differentiator and own the heck out of it.

- **Give consistent context**: Formally document your brand and get the whole team on board. Live and die by your messaging bible.

- **Sell the vision, not features**: The first job is to inspire prospects to see themselves in your story. Talk about features in the follow-up call.

- **Go multichannel and multi-touch**: Look for as many ways—and from as many different angles as possible—to get your brand in front of the market every day. Engage a branding and marketing firm full of creatives to help while you're taking care of the product.

How you present technology or data is critical. It certainly isn't child's play, but it can still be compelling and fun.

Glossary of Terms and Acronyms

ABM (Account-Based Marketing): A marketing approach that targets high-value accounts.

AI (Artificial Intelligence): The simulation of human intelligence in machines.

B2B (Business-to-Business): A company selling products or services to other businesses.

B2C (Business-to-Consumer): A company selling directly to consumers.

Big Ideas (Messaging Framework Category): Foundational messaging themes that shape brand identity.

Brand Bible: A comprehensive guide that defines a company's voice, messaging, and visual identity.

Brand Discovery: The process of uncovering a company's unique identity.

Cavebrain: The instinct-driven, survival-oriented nature of the brain that favors simple, immediate, and emotionally compelling messages over complex, data-heavy explanations.

Clarity: ensuring that messaging is easy to understand, free from jargon, and directly communicates the essential idea.

Cluster & Cull: A process of refining messaging by grouping similar concepts and eliminating unnecessary elements to ensure clarity and coherence.

Cluster-Thought: An overstuffed, unfocused message that crams multiple ideas, jargon, and technical details together in a way that overwhelms or confuses the audience, making it difficult for them to grasp the core point or takeaway; usually identified by several commas or clauses that result in a single sentence that wraps multiple lines on a page, or one in which you have to take a breath (like here) in order to read out loud and is typically the result of editing by committee.

Committed (Audience): Customers who have made a purchase decision and may advocate for your brand.

CTA (Call to Action): A phrase or button prompting the audience to take immediate action.

Dorsal Attention Network (DAN): The brain's focus system, responsible for goal-directed attention.

DHS (Department of Homeland Security): A U.S. government agency focused on national security.

Evaluating (Audience): Prospects comparing your offering against alternatives.

Empathy Marketing: A strategy that connects with audiences on an emotional level.

Ethos (Credibility Appeal): The use of credibility, trust, and expertise to persuade an audience, as identified by Aristotle.

Eusocial: A term used in biology to describe the highest level of social organization in certain animal species, particularly insects like ants, bees, or termites.

Focus: Directing attention to the most important aspect of a message at the right time.

FUD (Fear, Uncertainty, and Doubt): A marketing or sales tactic designed to create skepticism about competitors.

GTM (Go-To-Market Strategy): A business plan for launching a product or service.

Heart, Head, and Gut Model: A framework aligning with Aristotle's persuasion modes (Pathos, Logos, Ethos), categorizing messaging based on emotional, logical, and credibility-driven appeals.

Holistic Value: Showcasing the added benefits beyond the expected.

ICP (Ideal Customer Profile): A detailed description of the perfect customer for a business.

KPI (Key Performance Indicator): A measurable value demonstrating progress toward objectives.

Logos (Logical Appeal): The use of logic, data, and reason to persuade an audience, as identified by Aristotle.

Machine Learning (ML): A subset of AI that enables computers to learn from data.

Mantras (Messaging Framework Category): Short, repeatable phrases that reinforce brand messaging and reflect culture and character.

Marketing Funnel: A framework guiding potential customers from awareness to purchase.

Message Pyramid/Messaging Framework: A structured framework for developing consistent, first-principle messaging.

ML (Machine Learning): A subset of AI that enables computers to learn from data.

Nerd: Traditionally defined as a person who is highly intellectual, passionate, or deeply knowledgeable about a particular subject or field, often to the point of obsession. The term has evolved from a pejorative stereotype of socially awkward individuals with niche interests into a badge of honor for those who embrace curiosity, technical expertise, and deep thinking.

In this book, Nerd is used as a term of empowerment—referring to anyone who is passionate about their craft, whether in technology, marketing, cybersecurity, or beyond. It's not about social awkwardness; it's about embracing intelligence, creativity, and the ability to communicate complex ideas in a way that makes them accessible and engaging.

Periodic Table of Big Ideas: A system for categorizing different types of brand positioning and messaging strategies, akin to the periodic table of elements.

Pathos (Emotional Appeal): The use of emotion to persuade an audience, as identified by Aristotle.

PLG (Product-Led Growth): A business model that relies on product usage to drive customer acquisition.

Proof Points (Messaging Framework Category): Quantitative and qualitative validation of a message's claims.

ROI (Return on Investment): A metric for evaluating the efficiency of an investment.

Rule of Three: A writing technique that makes concepts more memorable.

SEO (Search Engine Optimization): Techniques used to improve a website's visibility in search results.

SOC (Security Operations Center): A centralized team that monitors and responds to cybersecurity threats.

Story Stacks: A technique of layering messaging inputs from different categories to create more cohesive narratives.

Storytelling: The practice of using narratives to make information more engaging and memorable.

Technical Evangelist: A person responsible for promoting a company's technical innovations.

Unaware (Audience): Prospects who don't recognize yet that they have a problem.

Value (Messaging Framework Category): The core benefits a company offers its audience.

You: Now a Nerd That Talks Good!!

Additional Reading and References

Here is a list of some books, papers, and other media that have informed this book. Some are referenced and others are sources that I think a tech or marketing nerd could dig into (in no particular order).

◯◯

Aristotle's Pathos, Logos, Ethos

The *Art of Rhetoric* by Aristotle

An essential work on persuasive communication.

https://classics.mit.edu/Aristotle/rhetoric.html

"The Differences between Speech and Writing: Ethos, Pathos, and Logos" by Robert J. Connors

Journal article that explores how speech and written copy need to leverage different rhetorical techniques.

https://doi.org/10.2307/356398

"Using Rhetorical Strategies for Persuasion"

A practical guide to understanding and applying rhetorical strategies.

https://owl.purdue.edu/owl/general_writing/academic_writing/establishing_arguments/rhetorical_strategies.html

Maslow's Hierarchy of Needs

Motivation and Personality by Abraham H. Maslow

Foundational text introducing the hierarchy of needs theory.

"A Theory of Human Motivation" by Abraham H. Maslow

Maslow's original paper outlining his motivational theory.

https://psychclassics.yorku.ca/Maslow/motivation.htm

Individual in Society: A Textbook of Social Psychology by David Krech, Richard S. Crutchfield, and Egerton L. Ballachey

Source of the visual inspiration for the messaging importance over time.

Drive: The Surprising Truth About What Motivates Us by Daniel H. Pink

Explores modern perspectives on motivation beyond Maslow's theory.

"What Maslow's Hierarchy Won't Tell You About Motivation" by Susan Fowler

Discusses the relevance of Maslow's theory in contemporary marketing.

https://hbr.org/2014/11/what-maslows-hierarchy-wont-tell-you-about-motivation

Persuasion

Science of Persuasion Episodes on *Hidden Brain*

A podcast episode exploring persuasive techniques.

Part 1: https://hiddenbrain.org/podcast/persuasion-part-1

Part 2: https://hiddenbrain.org/podcast/persuasion-part-2

Classical Advertising Methods

Scientific Advertising by Claude C. Hopkins

A pioneering work on effective advertising techniques.

Ogilvy on Advertising by David Ogilvy

Insights from one of the most influential figures in advertising.

Multiple works articles by E. St. Elmo Lewis on advertising principles:

- **"Catch-Line and Argument,"** *The Book-Keeper* 15 (1903)

- **"Side Talks about Advertising,"** *The Western Druggist* 21 (1899): 65-66.

- *Financial Advertising* (Levey Bros., 1908)

- **"The Duty and Privilege of Advertising a Bank,"** *The Bankers' Magazine* 78 (1909): 710-11

Joseph Campbell's Hero's Journey and Storytelling

The Hero with a Thousand Faces by Joseph Campbell

Introduces the monomyth concept and its applications.

The Writer's Journey: Mythic Structure for Writers by Christopher Vogler

Seminal book that applies Campbell's theories to storytelling and screenwriting.

"How Stories Shape the Meaning of Brands"

Examines how the Hero's Journey framework can enhance marketing narratives.

https://brandingstrategyinsider.com/how-stories-shape-the-meaning-of-brands/

Building a StoryBrand: Clarify Your Message So Customers Will Listen by Donald Miller

A good, basic exploration of the hero's journey and application to marketing stories.

Anything by professor Jonathan Gottschall, particularly:

- His TedX Talk **"The Storytelling Animal"**: https://www.youtube.com/watch?v=Vhd0XdedLpY

- His book *The Storytelling Animal: How Stories Make Us Human*

Interdisciplinary Connections

Thinking, Fast and Slow by Daniel Kahneman

Explores the dual systems that drive the way we think.

Made to Stick: Why Some Ideas Survive and Others Die by Chip Heath and Dan Heath

Identifies the traits that make ideas memorable and impactful.

Hit Makers: How to Succeed in an Age of Distraction by Derek Thompson

Fascinating book on trends and why some things "go viral" and others don't.

"Politics and the English Language" by George Orwell

A must-read for anyone in media, PR, or marketing—covering how language changes can influence and control populations.

https://www.orwellfoundation.com/the-orwell-foundation/orwell/essays-and-other-works/politics-and-the-english-language

Evolutionary Psychology: A Primer, by Leda Cosmides and John Tooby

An introduction to the field of evolutionary psychology.

Technical Marketing and Communications

Developer Marketing Does Not Exist by Adam DuVander

Slightly reverse perspective from this book. Focused more on how marketers can reach developers.

Make it Punchy: How to Write Simple Tech Messaging That Wins Hearts, Minds & Markets by Emma Stratton

One of the smartest B2B tech marketers out there.

Architecting Success: The Art of Soft Skills in Technical Sales: Connect to Sell More by Evgeniy Kharam

A practical, career-focused approach to learning how to speak more clearly in highly technical situations, like sales and product marketing.

Acknowledgments and Thanks

Thank you to the following great communicators for sitting with me and sharing your insights and validating my crazy thoughts:

- **Rina Atienza**—Follow her Newsletter *Holy Hand Grenades* at holyhandgrenades.substack.com

- **Stephen Houraghan**—I highly recommend checking out his course at Brand Master Academy (brandmasteracademy.com) for an introduction to effective branding.

- **Joel Klettke**—Learn more about Joel at his websites (joelklettke.com and bestlookingmanintheworld.com).

- **Adam Shostack**—Teacher, threat researcher, and nerd that talks good (even if he doesn't think so). Check out his books and courses at Shostack + Associates (shostack.org).

Thank you to my many cheerleaders, beta-readers, clients, and startup mentees for providing me with valuable feedback about what worked (and what didn't).

Without you, this book would not have been possible.

To listen to my conversations with other nerds that talk good, subscribe to the podcast

Nerds That Talk Good

On this show, I hand the mic over to guest nerds who share their secrets to great communication in their respective fields.

HOSTED BY

JOEL BENGE

FIND IT AT **nerdthattalksgood.com/podcast**

Continue Your Nerd Journey

MORE RESOURCES, TRAININGS, COACHING AVAILABLE AT

MessageSpecs.com

CONNECT WITH **JOEL BENGE**

in linkedin.com/in/joelmbenge

🦋 bsky.app/profile/nerdthattalksgood.com

THANK YOU FOR READING!

If you enjoyed *Be a Nerd That Talks Good*, please leave a review on Goodreads or on the retailer site where you purchased this book.

www.ingramcontent.com/pod-product-compliance
Lightning Source LLC
Chambersburg PA
CBHW071558210326
41597CB00019B/3308